A Wounded Lion Roars Again

BY
—

MONIQUE C. PHILIPS

as told to Kate Kleinsasser

DEDICATION

To my late mother, my motivation and inspiration.
To my child, my freedom son and best friend.
To Grace Troyer, my grace of God on earth.
To Kate Kleinsasser, my light at the end of the tunnel.
Ultimately, to Jesus, my own miracle worker.

TABLE OF CONTENTS

ACKNOWLEDGMENTS

I want to give a special appreciation to the individuals who took their time to say, "Monique, we are here for you to support you and show you love." Being helped freely is a very new thing for me, but it is my reality. I want to express a special thanks to the ones who assisted in publishing my story. Thank you to Kate Kleinsasser for typing the manuscript as I shared my story. Thank you, Andrew Weaver, for organizing and editing the content, and Ruthie Leibee for your help organizing the manuscript. Thank you, Claire Mahrefat, for your beautiful work designing the cover and formatting my book.

In all my dilemmas, I have learned to return all glory to the main pilot of my life, the general commander and director of my roller coaster journey. He who spared my life through rough roads and razor paths is the Author of my life. He is my Way Paver, Miracle Worker, and the greatest Judge who set me free from all accusations of my heart's imprisonment. He is the Light in the darkness. He gave me confidence, and now I live as the evidence. He brought me from darkness to light, and this is what I want the world to know. I give all the glory to the King of all kings and the Lion of the tribe of Judah. To Jesus Christ alone, I dedicate this book to open a new chapter of life in Christ.

INTRODUCTION

by Grace Troyer

What felt like an ordinary day of mediating for women in a refugee camp became a date indelibly etched in my memory when I met Monique for the first time. I couldn't even guess at the deep fear, desperation, and heartache she lived with. That evening, I found her alone in a dark tent, worshiping through song. As I listened to the words drifting through the dark night, "You are great, yes You are; Holy One, walked upon the sea…" I caught a glimpse of the holy hopes, dreams, and miracles in the heart of this special woman.

Monique is a big-hearted woman who meets no stranger, bringing the lonely into her already large circle of friends. Visit her, and she'll sweep you up in a giant hug and spin you around. Then she'll dish out heaps of Nigerian *fufu* and fish soup and urge you to eat it all. If you don't, she'll fuss about Americans who hardly eat anything and tell you Africans are strong because they eat *fufu*.

She carries heavy loads on her head with ease, but as you watch how she cares for her son, welcomes the stranger, and has faith to expect big things from God, you'll see her strength is not just physical. She has weathered unspeakably hard things in her life and is emerging strong and courageous. The stamina and determination of this woman are incredible, but the grace of God at work in her life is even more incredible.

While this book is Monique's story, it is also the story of God's redemptive heart. It has been my great privilege and honor to see the salvation of the Lord in her life. His ceaseless pursuit of Monique strengthens my faith in His desire for all people to be redeemed to Him. Even in the darkest chapters, a thread of gold is woven into her story—God relentlessly pursuing her, rescuing her, and bringing her back to Himself even when she was weary and spent.

No matter your story, God is pursuing you as well. As you read Monique's story, let the reality of Jesus' redeeming love encourage your faith that none of us are beyond His reach or below His pursuit. He is a God of miracles.

Narrow Escape

I walked into the beautiful European airport in the city, feeling trapped as I shuffled between my two traffickers. A black woman led the way, and as instructed, I followed her closely and copied all her actions. A white woman walked close behind me, watching my every move and preventing my escape.

The two women had met me outside one of Europe's notorious refugee camps, convincing me to follow them by threatening to harm my friends. Having been trafficked for years, I knew what kind of people they were, and I knew what they intended to do to me. However, I felt trapped and helpless as I was repeatedly told that if I only cooperated with them, my friends—especially Gracia—would be safe. She worked inside the camp I had left, and I hadn't even said goodbye to her.

I knew I had to follow them without any struggle because I believed they had been sent by my madam, Madam Malus. I had seen firsthand how ruthless and deadly Madam Malus could be, so I took their threats very seriously. The women told me they would sell my child when I gave birth, and then I would be free to resume working for my madam.

I followed them numbly, thinking that I would figure out what to do when we reached our destination in Spain. One thing you shouldn't do is argue with traffickers when they are threatening someone you love. I knew they would hurt Gracia, the friend I cared most about in the world. She was the first one who had truly loved me after 12 years of violence and exploitation.

When I walked into the airport, I desperately scanned the crowd for white faces, hoping to see someone who would recognize my predicament and intervene to help me. The traffickers had told me how to scan my boarding pass, and I passed the first checkpoint without a problem. All the airport employees were just busy with their jobs, and no one recognized that I was being trafficked. People working in these places should be trained to be more observant. My heart broke in despair—nobody in that big European airport understood my body language or my silent cry for rescue.

When we reached the boarding gate, I was still doing as I had been told, copying the actions of the woman in front of me. An airline employee scanned my passport, glanced at me with a smile, and returned my documents to me as she said, "Enjoy your flight."

I was sure my life was over because no one understood what was happening to me. The traffickers had persuaded me to leave Europe with them by threatening the people I loved, and now I was falling straight into their hellish trap that I knew all too well.

Several officials were standing in the boarding tunnel as we boarded, and I saw that they were checking the passports of some of the passengers. I immediately felt that if they were security people, they might be the ones to help me.

My heart was pounding like a drum when I reached the officials, but they didn't ask to see my passport. In desperation, I stopped and handed my passport to one of them, forcefully pinching his hand as I did so. He didn't seem to notice my signal, so I scratched the back of his hand in a final plea for him to understand.

Then he realized that I needed something and lifted his face to look straight at me.

"What's wrong?" he asked, and his voice sounded kind.

I locked eyes with him, pleading silently for help. I could hardly breathe as the lives of my unborn child and me were in the balance.

"Come with me," said the official, and the two women who were trafficking me continued to board the plane, pretending they had nothing to do with me. They didn't know that I had discreetly alerted the European officials of my danger.

"You are safe here," the security men assured me after they had led me into a different room. "You can trust us to help you. Do you have anyone you want to contact? Is there anyone you can trust to help you?"

"There is a girl named Gracia," I told them.

They took me to the police headquarters, and I refused to go anywhere outside of that police station. They told me I was free to go, but I refused to leave. It was the only place I felt safe, and I wanted to stay there.

I felt better when they allowed me to stay. It's better to be in prison as a free person than to endure the life I was escaping. I felt safer there than anywhere in the world. The police gave me a small room with a bed, and I felt secure knowing the station was full of officers with guns. A kind person brought me some food, but I couldn't eat.

I couldn't sleep either, but I lay on the prison bed and tried to rest. My baby was very active within me, kicking as if he wanted to celebrate that we had escaped slavery and death.

I called my friend Gracia and was relieved to hear that she was okay. When I heard her voice over the phone, I relaxed a little. As long as my friends weren't harmed, there was no problem.

I had just left the refugee camp on the island where thousands of refugees flooded the shores, arriving on small rubber rafts from Turkey. They were smuggled to Europe by men on the Turkish border who often used guns to cram many desperate refugees onto small rubber rafts. Volunteers from several different organizations brought the refugees from the seaside to the camp, where many lived in small pop-up tents scattered everywhere. The camp had once been a prison, and to us, the island was still imprisoning us, keeping us from hope and a new future.

The government mostly didn't bother to help us, so I was grateful for the space and the food provided by the organizations. I was crammed into a small room with bunk beds with other pregnant women, but I had medical care and my basic needs met. I could sleep and wake up without anyone raping me, so I was grateful.

I wrote a lot while perched on my bunk in Section C, the space in the camp for pregnant women traveling alone. My pen hurried across the paper, trying to keep up with the flood of thoughts, memories, and emotions I was experiencing.

November 2017
Written in the Camp's Section C, Room 1
I bring my testimony and my story to the glory of God because my Bible made me understand that I shall overcome the devil by the blood of the Lamb and the words of my testimony. All of us are

running one heavenly race and will give an account of the flock that was handed to us and how we took care of them. A rich man on earth, with all he possesses, with the qualifications he has; will they take him to heaven? Or do you think it all ends here on earth?

It's appointed unto man to die once, and after that is judgment. I tell you, my dear reader and listener, after life here on earth, you and I will be facing the only God who is not biased or corrupt to face our judgment. You, as a president, governor, senator, chairman, counselor, judge, pastor, teacher, parent, landlord, landlady, preacher, or driver—have you taken a second to ask yourselves during the night what happens if you don't wake up the next morning?

God created us in His image and likeness. No child of God is meant to pass through this hell in life. His plans for us are good, not evil. Most situations we find ourselves in are not what God wants for us. Yet God will still turn the table around to give you a testimony because He will have mercy upon whom He will have mercy. God does not ask permission when He wants to bless you. No one decreases when God has increased, and no man speaks when God has not spoken.

In all situations, my brethren, give God thanks. Your thanks given in a bad condition can make things begin to happen. If you are happy, pray. If you are suffering, pray. During hardship, pray. In every situation, pray.

CHAPTER 1

Mother and I

My dear reader, my name is Monique, and I am from the Igbo tribe in Nigeria. The three main ethnic groups in Nigeria are the Igbo, Hausa, and Yoruba tribes. The Hausa are Muslim, while the Yoruba are mixed. My tribe speaks the Igbo language, and we are known for making money.

I was born in August 1993. I was raised by a single mother and never met my father In fact, I have no idea if he is even alive. My mother was the only family I knew or friend I had. She hid all details about my family and identity for personal reasons. I believe it was for the best.

Being an extremely protective parent, my mother told me I would become pregnant if I let a man touch me. If two men touched me, she said I'd have two pregnancies. Because I believed her, I would shout about pregnancy at school whenever a man touched me.

My mother also didn't want people to know I was a girl, so I would be protected from evil people who abuse women. She had me wear baggy clothes, and I played a lot with boys, although I stayed far enough away from them to avoid being touched by them.

One day, I asked my mother about my father. I was in primary school, and the children were talking about what their fathers bought for them. I complained to my mother at home, "My classmates are saying that their fathers buy them things. Where is my father to buy something for me?"

Mother shrewdly sent me to the shop with money to buy Coca-Cola and biscuits, and I was so excited that I forgot my curiosity about my father.

At that time, only rich people would drink malt with condensed milk. When I asked questions about my father, my mother told me not to ask her again, and she gave me malt and milk to distract me.

My mother named me Monique after a lady she knew who was decent, respectful, and intelligent, hoping I would be just like her when I grew up. Unfortunately, I became the opposite of her. Even when I was little, I was stubborn, and my mother told me that I was not like the other Monique.

Mother tried to make a normal and healthy life for me and looking back now, I understand how hard she worked to protect me. I cherish all the memories of her wise words and her good food.

Fufu is a staple that all Nigerians eat, whether rich or poor. We cannot do without it and usually eat it for lunch. It's solid food, so you will eat it and not be hungry for a long time. It is made of cassava or yam flour, and we cook it into a thick paste on the stove and eat it with our hands, dipping it into a sauce or soup to flavor it.

Ukwa is a Nigerian fruit known as breadfruit in English. It is usually a rich man's food, and we have many ways to prepare it. Some people just dry it, fry it, and chew it like peanuts. When you cook it, you add spices and vegetables. Some people just wash and boil it and eat it with sauce. My Mother wasn't wealthy, but she made breadfruit for me, and I loved it. She boiled it, added salt, and we ate it while drinking the water it was cooked in. My favorite way of eating it was cooking it and adding stockfish, pepper, red oil, and pumpkin. It became porridge, and we would eat it for lunch. This is often the most expensive plate at a restaurant.

Childhood can be a good memory for some people, while for others, something they don't want to talk about. Some children experience the best childhood, while others experience the opposite. Some get all the things they want, but their parents are not there for them. They will be left with nannies, and sometimes those nannies mistreat them.

Some children have no parents, are forced to work as little house helpers, and are not treated well. They must live to see what the future has for them. Some grow up with a single mother who gives them only what she feels they need and not what they want.

Some parents ask their kids questions about their daily activities. Others don't ask, and when the child musters the courage to say anything, the parents shut them up or don't give a listening ear when the child pours out his heart.

My mom was that kind of parent. She didn't want to talk or communicate much. I had many things to say to her, but she was naturally quiet and wouldn't speak. Usually, the only response to my questions was a proverb, and I was too small to understand proverbs or parables. My mother never played with

me, and she also taught me that tears were a sign of weakness and that I should never cry.

I asked her one day, "Why are some people suffering and some enjoying life?"

She replied, "They are suffering because they don't know God or don't believe in God. When you know and believe in God, you will know nothing is difficult for God to do."

Her answer confused me because I expected to hear that there are three categories of people in this life: the rich, the poor, and the middle class.

"Mother, how do you believe so much in God?" I asked.

"Blessed are those who believe without seeing," she answered.

I was as confused as before, but I know my mother was doing the best she knew to coach me to grow up in the fear of God. Maybe she forgot to warn me that wolves waited outside to devour me once she was gone.

"Mom, what happens to me if you die?" I asked.

"Nothing happens without God's consent," she said.

This is when she could have told me about other family members I could turn to—father, uncles, or aunties. But she told me nothing.

Mother said, "Someday, we will meet to part no more where death and sickness cannot touch us."

During all the years that I was molested, raped, and trafficked, I kept the hope of meeting my mother again where we won't be parted, so I can ask her the questions still in my mind.

Now that I am the mother of a young boy, I give him everything my mother gave me, and I add the listening and attention she missed during my childhood. I forgive my late mother for not listening to me or paying emotional attention. I know that deep down, she wanted me to be the strongest woman because she knew what awaited me if anything happened to her.

Mother, one of the most valuable things you taught me was never to be envious of anyone because the belly never shows what one ate. Being a single mother has taught me a great lesson; I would have reacted similarly to or worse than you did in the same circumstances. You had no one to rely on or talk with. I feel your pain now.

My mother wasn't educated, so she wanted me to pursue an education. Here I am with not much education either, but I wish I could study. Exposure and speaking out is therapy for one's soul. She had neither.

I have always had a mind to multiply money. I took 100 *naira* when I was a child, went to the market, and bought some garden eggs. I sold them and shared the money and profit with beggars at Saint Faith Cathedral Church. People who saw me sharing money with those beggars told my mom that I was stealing her money and sharing it with beggars and that her money would soon end.

Being a wise woman, she didn't shout or hit me. Instead, she observed me carefully and saw when I stole her 100 *naira*. She followed me one day and saw when I bought the garden eggs, sold them, and went to share with the beggars. I realized there was one extra beggar that day, but I had no idea it was my mother because she was wearing a large summer hat.

When I came back to the house, Mother cautioned me and said, "Helping is good, but stealing is bad. Don't steal to help; rather, help to stop stealing."

I told her I wanted to build a school or hospital in her name when I grew up. What shame I feel when I think of that now.

I can't boast of my house rent, much less a school or hospital for the poor.

Mother was a woman in her own world. She never gave me all I wanted, but she gave me the best I needed. I wasn't allowed to have candy and other sweets when I was young. She sent me to the best school to become a police officer when I grew up. My mother wanted me to protect the vulnerable and be a voice for the voiceless.

She was a reticent and self-isolated person, a God-fearing Christian woman. Despite all she experienced as a single mother and her difficult adulthood, she kept her faith in God.

I will forever remember when I asked her how she could still worship God in her situation.

She replied, "My daughter, even if we don't worship God, He will still be God. He won't change one bit, He won't be decreased, and His name will still be God. Come on, my daughter, join me to keep worshiping God!"

When I was about 10 years old, I dreamed about my future. In the dream, I was in a camp and inside a tent. A white girl came up to me and said, "What are you doing here? You are not supposed to be here since you're pregnant. Follow me."

I know God loves me and all His creatures. Whatever He does is good. He doesn't derive joy from seeing His children suffering. Before I was born, He knew what I would be. Twelve years being trafficked was like an eternity to me—but it took only a second for Him to turn everything around.

As a child, I kept praying when I saw my mother pray, and I did as she told me. But I knew deep down, she had many questions, but who could she ask? I knew she had lots of worries and fears, but who could she rely on? In my country of Nigeria, the poor have no voice or help to fight the oppressors.

My mother tried to be upright, do the right things, and stay safe from the known and unknown dangers. She was intelligent and wise, but she was also lonely and fearful. I understand now why she was isolated and afraid, but it didn't make sense to me then.

When I was seven years old, she forbade me to play with other children, so I tried to amuse myself with questions and answers and played with rubber bands.

My dearest Mother,

I just want to let you know that I remember all the things you tried to teach me when it seemed I wasn't listening. Your lessons keep ringing bells in my ears and mind, and I wish you could see how I am passing them on to my son, your grandson.

Mother, don't worry. I really understand your pains now. Seeing my son do only 1/10th of what I did, I feel pity for what I put you through. And yet, you didn't give up on me.

I love you.

CHAPTER 2

Childhood

I started primary school when I was only four years old, and I was the best student there. From the beginning, I was teaching the other children simple facts like 1+1 and 2+2. However, I had no friends at school. They called me a bastard because I did not have a daddy. My mother did her best to provide me with a good life and education.

I was an intelligent child and tried to trick my mother for my benefit. Some of the other children were often sick and received special treatment, so one day, I judged the time when Mother would come back from the market. Before she returned, I sat in the sun to make myself feel hot.

When Mother came home, I sat close to her, and she exclaimed, "Your body is hot!"

I was so excited because I thought she would give me malt and milk. Instead, she insisted that I take a bath first, and when I did, my body cooled down. I declared that I was sick with a fever, but she knew I had just been standing under the sun.

I also loved to trick my mother because she couldn't read. When we would walk down the street, she would ask me to read the signs. I would say, "It says Monique Street," or, "The sign says Monique is a very nice girl."

She laughed and said, "Monique, Monique, Monique... are you really that popular?"

I climbed mango trees often, threw stones, and fought with boys in the street. My mother even had two trees cut down so I would stop climbing them.

There is a forbidden tree in Nigeria called the African star apple. People say it is the tree Eve took the fruit from. There are many myths about this tree, and no one climbs it or throws stones at it, as it is greatly respected. We had a big one close to our house, and I would shinny up the tree and fall asleep in the branches because it was so huge. That tree became my favorite escape place. I put a rope up for myself, and I loved it up there away from the world, covered in leaves, gorging on the fruit, and throwing the seeds down on unsuspecting passersby.

The other refuge I had was a big gutter. When my mother would punish me, I would escape and run into this gutter, where soft sand had been washed in by the rain. I would lie on the sand and even fall asleep there. The gutter and the star apple tree were my two childhood apartments.

Some people in Nigeria throw sacrifices into the street to appease curses. I would find their money, eggs, peanuts, Coca-Cola, or chewing gum and run into my gutter to eat them. Nigerian mothers always tell their children never to pick money off the street or else they will turn into a goat. I picked up all the money I found and never turned into a goat; I merely got richer.

One day, a chicken was running around our space, so I threw a stone and killed it. I didn't intend to kill it, but I had a good aim. The lady who owned it was a witch doctor, and it was her chicken. She was angry and came to tell my mother that the chicken I killed was for a sacrifice. I escaped to my private tree until the fuss passed over. No one could beat me there, and that tree felt like my real family.

I was always looking for ways to make money as a child. My playmates told me witch doctors used lizards for their fetishes. Since our neighbor was a witch doctor, I started going on lizard hunts and caught all the lizards I could. The bigger ones were more valuable, but they would try to snap at us, so we learned to hold them behind the head. The males had red heads and were more expensive. My friend helped me and guided my hand until I swiftly caught them and put them into my lizard bucket. We also gathered the lizard eggs for the witch doctor. She bought them from me for five *naira* per lizard.

I was so happy to make money, but Mother found out because she watched everything I did. Since she didn't want me mingling with children, she would find my bucket of lizards and smoke them with fire until they died or escaped because of the smoke.

Although I did all these things as an innocent child, many of my actions hurt my mother. I wonder now what was going through her mind then. She must have been wondering, "How did I become the mother of this child? What did I do that God cursed me with such a burden as Monique? Why is she so opposite of me?"

When I was six years old, I was having some dreams, and Mother thought I was demon-possessed. She took me to one of the "white robe" churches to cast out the demon. They had me kneel while they yelled and rang bells to cast it out. They took a live pigeon and beat me with it until the poor bird died.

After that, I stopped telling my mother when I felt something spiritual, so she thought I was delivered from the demon. However, I was still fascinated with the supernatural and wanted to participate in the yearly masquerade festival. In eastern Nigeria, where we lived, ladies were not supposed to be involved in masquerades. Being stubborn and stupid, I dressed like a boy to join the masquerade festival when I was about 9 years old. It was all about magic tricks, and everyone came to perform. We ate, drank, and danced. The performers were called spirits, and women were not allowed to follow them. Some of the masqueraders brought fire from their mouths or laid eggs. The witch doctors, using voodoo, followed the performers to give them power. Some people see it as just a cultural practice, but I think it is spiritual also.

I felt like the traditionalists were better than the Nigerian Christians because I don't like two-faced knives. I could see what kind of people the traditionalists were, but many Christians were hypocrites and tried to deceive others.

One day, my mother suddenly packed all our essential belongings into bags. She carried one bag on her head and two in her hand, and we left the only home I knew. She didn't tell me why we were leaving or explain where we were going. I was most heartbroken that we had to leave our TV behind.

We jumped on motorbikes and buses and traveled from village to village for several days. We finally stopped somewhere where Mother found an abandoned building we could stay in. I still don't exactly know why we suddenly fled our home and moved into an abandoned building, but I know you don't leave your comfort zone unless something is chasing you. My mother must have known about some danger that threatened us.

Mother managed to sell flour in the new village to earn some money. Anywhere she stopped, she created business. She also sold fried snacks on the street, and I helped her by tying shut the little bags of food.

My mother made *akara*: beans soaked in water, blended with onions, salt, pepper, and oil, then fried in balls. The vendor who fries the *akara* always fries it together with potato, yam, and plantain and serves it all together. It is sold around bus stops and other busy places. Another food that can provide a business is called *buff-buff*. It is flour mixed with sugar and salt, and you add water and oil and fry them in oil.

Slowly, Mother started making the uncompleted building into a shelter for us, trying to make some protection from the rain. I was angry and sad because I didn't know what had happened or why we were running. Mother was afraid of something, so we traveled from place to place until we arrived in Lagos, the largest city in Nigeria. It seems now like my mother had her own story of escaping captivity, but she never breathed a word about it.

Today, I am proud to be the daughter of a woman of few words who answered my questions with parables. All that I use in my daily life, I learned from her. Mother taught me how to live if life gets tough. She showed me how to:

1. Be brave
2. Be content with what I have
3. Make decisions
4. Never be lazy
5. Stand upright

6. Know when to say yes and no
7. Be optimistic
8. Trust in God
9. Be independent

She always said, "A living dog is better than a dead lion."
Another favorite saying was, "P.U.S.H. Pray Until Something Happens."

My mother also told me, "Put your hopes in God and not men because men will fail you."

"When you wake up in the morning, pinch yourself. If you are alive, there is hope."

Although my mother didn't know how to read or write, she was eager to hear the contents of the Bible and asked me to read it aloud for her. She listened more than she spoke, while I am quite the opposite and talk a lot.

I was twelve years old when we arrived in Lagos. By then, I was used to surviving from bush to bush, covered with mosquitoes, so when I saw a big city full of houses with actual lights, I was so happy. My mother, however, was always unhappy and unpleasant there. I believe she was trying to escape an impending doom and sensed what would happen next.

I look back and feel her pain now. I understand what she must have been fighting. But back then, I was only a child wanting malt and milk. I didn't know my life would soon fall apart into a million pieces.

I was 13 years old when my life changed suddenly, and my hell on earth began.

When I returned from school one day, I saw my mother lying on the couch. She was foaming at the mouth, and her tongue was hanging out. A cup with some liquid was on the table close to her.

A lady came out of the house and introduced herself as Madam Barine. She told me my mother was feeling sick and couldn't talk, and that I should go with her.

I was happy that I was finished with school and went with Madam Barine with no worries. She took me to her own house and told me that she had been my neighbor and that she was my mother's friend. Being very young and inexperienced, I believed her. Later that night, Madam Barine told me that my mother was dead, and I could not go home.

I started crying, but I couldn't believe my mother was actually dead.

Madam Barine acted kind to me and promised me that she would take care of me. She said she would take me to a different place since I would miss my mother so much.

I was too young to realize that my mother had been murdered and that I was being kidnapped.

Soon I asked to leave the house and go back to my mother.

"Don't worry," Madam Barine said. "I will take you there."

I fell asleep that night in her house, and when I woke up, I felt like I was living a dream. I still didn't believe my mother was dead, so Madam Barine took me to a large morgue that morning. We went in and walked past so many bodies until, at last, I saw my mother's face. I asked Madam Barine for her phone and took a photo because I thought that, when I grew up, I would come back and give my mother a proper burial.

We then went back to my mother's house, and I took her photo from inside a book to remember her face. When I saw the cross on the wall, I tore it down on an impulse and broke it. I also tore her Bible into pieces and declared, "I will never, never worship this God my mother worshiped."

Where was the God my mother believed in?

We went back to Madam Barine's house, and she started making travel plans for me. She took me to Ghana on a bus and dropped me off at a family's house as a working slave.

Death is inevitable. We all shall die someday, but what happens after our death is a mystery we cannot know. When a person dies, it affects people around them. When a mother dies, the husband carries the burden. But if an orphan like my mother dies, what becomes of the child she left behind with no family? Think about it.

First, the child becomes vulnerable to everything and anything. With no family, the child enters the streets, eats from the slums, and is raped repeatedly by hoodlums. There are no quality services for children, no social services, no helpers. Instead, an orphan, as I had become, gets exploited.

No wonder I began to ask God, "Where are you?"

CHAPTER 3

Becoming Sarah

Losing my mother was not just one sad event; it was the beginning of a new life of hardship and pain with no father, siblings, uncles, or aunties, whether good or wicked. It was just me and me alone, and I became vulnerable for the vultures to feed on.

I was taken away by a group of traffickers whose boss is a woman, a very dangerous serpent. When I was taken to Ghana, my journey started like Joseph's in the Bible. I was meant to be a housemaid, but God, in His infinite mercy, touched the couple's heart to treat me like their own child. My new boss's pastor told her that I had a good spirit and that if she treated me well, she would be able to have a child of her own.

For three years, I stayed with this couple in Ghana. They treated me well, considering that my life would soon take a turn for the worse. At least they gave me food.

Early each morning, I had to clean the house. When that was finished, I would go to the market to sell water and snacks from a basket I carried on my head. I had the gift of selling faster than anyone else there. I would find a place with loud music and dance very well, and people bought more from me. I loved dancing so much.

Everything seemed to be going well until one of my boss's family members came to visit. The rest of the family left the house one day, and this man entered the room. He said, "Don't worry, I don't want to touch your vagina; I want to touch your anus." He then anally raped me.

I grabbed a clothes iron and struck him hard with the cord, and he fell. I ran out of the house and waited and waited for the family to come home so I could tell them he was a beast.

When my boss came back, I tried to explain what had happened. From then on, I was locked inside the compound.

The guy who had assaulted me left, but they did not report his crime to the authorities because he was a family member. I was suffering severe pain because of what he had done to me, so my bosses gave me some pain pills. They warned me that they would kill me if I ever breathed a word to anyone about what had happened to me.

I believed their threats, living in fear and not speaking a word about the incident until finally, my bosses had children of their own.

Madam Barine, who had been with me when my mother died, had sold me to this family and kept the money for herself. When my madam found out about this, Madam Barine came to Ghana at her bidding. I didn't know at this time that I was being controlled by someone I didn't know, Madam Malus. Madam Barine came to the house where I worked and told me her boss was summoning me to a better place. I packed my bags, said goodbye, and jumped into a car with her.

The car took us to a place that looked like a standard guesthouse. Madam Barine took me inside, where she and a man took me into a room.

I was taken to experience what they called "initiation circumcision." I had entered a brothel, although I didn't know what it was. I thought it was a regular apartment. It had many rooms, and they were full of girls. I heard screaming from the other rooms, so I concluded they were being raped.

I was just 13 years old.

My life changed when they took me there. I hoped it was a nightmare and that I would soon wake up, but it was real. My traffickers told me my name had been changed and that I had lost my identity. From now on, I would no longer be Monique, but my name would be Sarah, a name Madam had chosen for me.

My first initiation was with a native doctor who forcefully had sex with me in that room. He used a white handkerchief to clean up the bloodstain, which he put in a bowl with some liquid concoction and forced me to drink. I tried to resist, but four men held me down. Although I hit hard and had good aim, I couldn't do anything against four men.

Then they started cutting my face for an identity ritual. I was told, "Your vagina belongs to your madam. Whatever goes into it belongs to her. Your vagina is her property. You are one of her investments."

As they cut my face, they asked, "What is your name?"

"Sarah," I said.

"Who are you working for?"

"Madam Malus."

From that moment, I had a new identity. I also had a headache. My captors said I shouldn't worry; I was only feeling ill because my identity had changed. From that day on, I was Sarah. It was a new name, but it had a spiritual attachment. Madam controlled all her girls by voodoo rituals using the name she gave them. She could control us with this name no matter where we went.

While there in Ghana, I moved into the brothel where Madam Barine had taken me and worked for one year. After the initiation, I knew I was done and felt hopeless. The clients were very old men who wanted young girls. In my year at that brothel, I never saw the other girls in the house, although I heard shouting and screaming every day from other rooms. I was locked inside my room all the time. It had a bathroom and a bed. The head of house brought food twice a day. There was a window, but it had bars, so there was no way of escaping.

This brothel was the initiation place for all the girls working for Madam. It was our breaking in. I had a television in my room that I watched between clients. In prison, you just sit there alone and are happy when you get to see someone. In the brothel, it was the opposite—any interaction with people meant suffering.

I had a Catholic rosary around my neck from my mother. One day, a client tore it while having sex with me, and the beads scattered everywhere. That rosary felt like the only evidence of God I still had, and I told myself it was good that a client broke it so I could challenge God and see what He would do for me.

Madam Barine worked for Madam Malus, but she wasn't taking the trafficked girls straight to a brothel as Madam Malus wanted. As she had done to me, she would take girls to a different house after kidnapping them and then sell them for her profit. She also conspired with a hospital that would tell the parents that their child in the hospital had died, and then they would kidnap and traffic the children.

When my madam realized that Madam Barine had taken me to a house, they quarreled about me. Madam Barine came and told me that I needed to go back to Nigeria with her. I knew that my life was changing again and that I was under the control of other people.

Later in life, I realized that Madam Barine had shown me a kindness by taking me to the family I worked for. She had been charged to take me straight to the "initiation circumcision" brothel after they killed my mother and kidnapped me. If my boss's relative had succeeded in raping me vaginally, Madam would have killed everyone involved with me. My first vaginal rape had to be done by a native doctor as part of a ritual, else I would be useless to them. The first vaginal blood goes to Madam, and she uses it for spiritual fortification and control. It also increases the protection she has. As you can see, her business was run by witchcraft.

People ask why I didn't simply run away. Why didn't I escape? Why didn't I report to the police? It was not so simple.

In the meantime, I had my own questions.

"Where is the God who formed me before I was born?"

I knew the answers from my mother's teaching. Before I was born, God already knew what I would be. My mother taught me the story of Joseph. She said, "Joseph went from prison to palace, but how long did the prison last? Before prison, he was betrayed by his own siblings and was sold by them. What was so heartbreaking was the emotional murder as he was accused by his master's wife of something he never did. Do you know how many long days, months, and years it all lasted? Finally, when he interpreted a dream for one of the king's servants, also in prison, the servant was released. Why didn't he immediately tell the king about Joseph? God had His plans, and His ways are far different from those of man. At the blessed time—the right moment—the king had the dream. When no one could interpret it, Joseph was indeed remembered."

My late mother was clever with her few words, God-fearing and full of wisdom. I started trying to honor her words in my life. Life mistreated me so badly that I should have questioned God, but who am I to question Him? A lot of us ask, "God, where are you?" The answer: God is everywhere—He is omnipresent. If I stop praising Him, He will still be God. Just because He has not answered you yet, does not mean he doesn't answer prayer. He is the God of all flesh, and there is nothing too impossible for Him to do. He is the Author and Finisher of our life, the Master Planner.

When I was small, I asked a question of my late mother because she liked preaching and was the very churchy type. I asked her, "Why are most Christians poor and the unbelievers rich?"

As she often did, my mother answered me with a question, "He who created the ocean that has all the entire schools of fish in it, is He poor?"

I said no, but I didn't fully understand at the time.

May the soul of my late mother rest in peace. She did her best to raise me before death took her, and she taught me to be content with whatever I had. She said, "Never envy anyone. Do not wish to be who you are not, for that leads to stealing. Do not boast, for everything on earth can vanish.

"Be yourself, my daughter, and it shall be well with you."

CHAPTER 4

Bandaged Beggar

The head of house came to my room at the brothel one day, and he told me to leave my room for the first time in about a year. I followed him out and was surprised to see Madam Barine in the reception area.

"How are you doing, Sarah?" she asked, but I was unable to reply. My spirit had been utterly broken from a year of sexual slavery inside that small room.

The traffickers had crushed me inside and robbed me of my childhood. While I should have been going to school and laughing with my friends, I was locked in a room and sold for the pleasure of depraved old men. How could I speak again?

My life with my mother had included poverty and difficulties, but it had also had happiness and contentment. Now, I was treated worse than an animal. I was an object with no more life than a stone. I was still a child, but I could never climb a tree or play with other children again.

Ignoring my silence, Madam Barine told me to come with her. I obeyed, too broken to even ask where we were going. She announced that she was taking me back to Nigeria, and I wondered if that was good news or bad. My life in Nigeria had never been as horrible as the past year in Ghana, so I was hopeful that I was leaving this life behind. Little did I realize, Ghana was only the opening chapter in a book of horrors.

While we traveled across Togo and Benin, back to my home country on a bus, Madam Barine kept trying to make conversation with me. She asked me how I was and how the brothel had been, but I didn't answer her. What do you say to someone who asks what it was like to be a sex slave?

When we arrived back in Nigeria, Madam Barine took me to a large warehouse in Lagos and told the men there, "I brought Sarah."

I looked around the warehouse and saw a lot of children, so I felt a little hope and relief. It was evening time, and the boss of the house had been expecting me and welcomed me. The building was large and full of bunk beds. The head of house told me to thank God that I could be with other children.

I didn't understand what was happening, but I had reached the second level of my captivity.

We had to sleep two in a bed. The girl I shared a bed with told me that she was an orphan and someone sold her to Madam from an orphanage, telling the orphanage that she died. We were always hungry, so I sometimes shared my food with her. She cried every night, and it disturbed me. I had stopped crying in Ghana.

One girl, Maryanne, made a Catholic altar to pray and do the rosary. She always told me, "Sarah, come, let's pray! Let's share the Word of God and pray!"

"I don't ever want to hear that out of your mouth again," I told her angrily. "Your name is Maryanne, which is like Mary in the Bible, and still you are here in this place? What good are your prayers?"

Although I refused to join, about half the children would stand and read some prayers and then kneel to pray.

My first job at the new place was to beg together with the other children. The heads of the house put large bandages on our bodies to make it look like we had sickness or broken limbs, then paraded us around to beg for alms. We were a group of approximately 50-70 children, and because we looked pitiful, many people gave us money. The men who pushed us around on wheelchairs to beg during the day raped us as they wanted at night.

I couldn't sleep, asking myself, "Where is my mother? Why did she die? Where is the God she served? Can't her God save her daughter from this?"

When the children cried, I tried to console them and told them tears wouldn't solve their problems.

One evening after we returned from a day of begging, the men were busy counting the money, so I saw my chance and ran out the door. I grabbed the handle of a nearby moving pickup in the street and held on for dear life. When the truck halted, I climbed in the back of another pickup, and when that stopped, I found another bus carrying tomatoes to ride.

Looking for a safe place, I slept in a motor park like a mechanic workshop. Four men found me there, and they all raped me. I passed out under their attack, and when I woke up, I was on a busy road that I didn't recognize. Some people found me on the road and took me to the police.

When I was at the police station, the officers asked me who I had run from, and I told them the truth, thinking they would protect me. I told them Madam Malus wanted to kill me, and I saw them glance at each other as if they knew that name. The next thing I knew, one of the men from the warehouse had come to pick me up. He took me back to the warehouse and asked Madam if they should kill me. She must have told them not to kill me, but they beat me mercilessly all over my body, including my head, covering me with bruises.

The children all pitied me and warned me not to attempt escape because another girl who tried had been killed.

Everything about that life was horrible. I went out during the day in a wheelchair, pretending to be handicapped, and came back to be raped by a politician or another client who was old enough to be my father. By the time I experienced all that, no evil could surprise me anymore except the witchcraft I would soon encounter.

The men in charge raped us, but they also made money by allowing their friends to rape us in the bathroom. We were forced to submit to all forms of rape. Some of them made us hold their semen in our mouths. One time, I couldn't take it anymore and bit a man very hard.

As punishment, I was tortured without mercy in front of the other children to teach them a lesson. My captors heated nails red-hot on the stove and shoved them into my legs. I still have the scars from those puncture wounds.

They told me, "Your job was to satisfy your client, not hurt him. You may only hurt them if they ask you to do it."

The other children cried in terror and sympathy to see me tortured like that, but there was one girl there who never cried. She never showed weakness, and she was the meanest person there. One day, our traffickers took her and me and another friend to a party for a senator. They took just my friend and a boy into another room. Being an inquisitive person, I watched through the keyhole to see what they were doing. They tied the girl down and put something in her mouth to muffle her screams. I was pressed against the door and squinting to see through the keyhole, and I watched in horror as they cut off her breasts. I never saw her again.

When I realized what they were doing, I ran out of the house and into the street because I was petrified they might do the same to me. After running away, I came back to my senses and realized I could be killed for leaving. Instead of going back to the party, I returned to the warehouse, and they chained me down. My boss, the head of house, called Madam and told her that I had run away again. She asked to speak to me on the phone and asked why I had run away. I told her I had seen them killing a girl and was frightened. Madam talked to the guys again, but I don't know what was said; I just know they didn't kill me that time.

The traffickers did not allow us children to be friends with each other. If they even saw us talking amongst ourselves, they would flog us. Despite their beatings, three of us girls, all orphans, got to know each other better.

Some women were paid to come to cook for us, and we ate only once a day. Sometimes when we were begging, we were given some biscuits or snacks, and we could eat that food at night in our beds. Many of the children tried to run away, but the traffickers didn't hesitate to kill them if they were caught. I had learned that escape was hopeless, but I lay awake at night

trying to think of a way to run away or kill myself. I felt like I was living in a nightmare most of the time.

Nigeria is a corrupt country where only the richest are heard. If you have the right connections, you or your family won't go to jail. With just one phone call to the right person, you can get out of police custody. Some of the girls had been arrested, but the police themselves handed the girls back to their madams. If you choose to continue running, you could pay with your life, or they might choose to harvest your most sensitive organs, like kidneys. If they spare your life, they might share nude pictures or videos of you on Facebook and other social media. If the head of house doesn't kill you when you try to flee, the oath of secrecy will kill you. This oath happens in the beginning when you take the voodoo fortification process, and when you escape, Madam can use it to kill you slowly.

I was beaten mercilessly and begged for death, but death never came. I even tried to disobey my late mother, who had taught me it was always wrong to take my own life, regardless of the circumstances. She said that if God wanted my life to end, He had ways to do that. However, in total despair, I tried to take my own life.

When my childhood was robbed of me, and my life changed, I just wanted it all to end, but I had already learned that I couldn't run away. There seemed to be no way out of my predicament. That's when I first thought about killing myself by drinking kerosene. We used kerosene in our lamps, our cooking stoves, and for starting fires, so it was common in every home. I found some in the kitchen for the kerosene stove, and I drank from the gallon jug right there in the kitchen.

After drinking it, I patiently waited for death to come, to join my mother. Although I knew this was a painful way to kill myself, I was willing to endure the stomach pain if I could just die.

Soon the tummy pain started, but I was happy because death was coming, although gradually. Some of the other girls noticed I was sick, and they notified the guys in the house. I told the girls to shut up, but it was too late. I was sitting against the wall waiting for death when the men of the house came. They made me open my mouth and smelled the kerosene on my breath. When they angrily slapped me, I didn't even care. I was happy that their slapping was the last hard thing I would ever endure.

But the men weren't giving up so easily. They forced red oil into my mouth, and one of them called our madam to inform her that I smelled like kerosene, and they suspected I had drunk some. Madam Malus told them to call the house doctor, the personal doctor that checks the girls at the brothel. When he arrived, he told the men to give me some medicine which I refused to take.

Although I resisted, they forced the medication through my throat. I slept it off, and when I woke up, I was expecting to be in another world. To my dismay, I found myself in the same spot, feeling healthier than before.

Most houses in Nigeria have a well where they fetch water, so in my disappointment and despair after the kerosene episode, I decided to kill myself by jumping into the well outside. I walked to the well and hurled myself into the black hole in the ground. While falling into the darkness, my clothes snagged on a step and caught me. I found myself hanging suspended above the water, still alive.

At that time, all of us girls working were living in the hallway on bunk beds. The other girls were all screaming when they saw me jump, so the man of the house came and called for help. He summoned the Hausa people from the tribe that traditionally dig wells. One of the Hausa men climbed down into the well with a rope. When he had fastened it around me, the men on the surface pulled me out.

Then the head of house beat me mercilessly with a *koboko*, a whip used by the military made from animal skins. My body was still wet from the well, and the whip stung terribly on my skin. My whole body was black with bruises.

It felt like death was so far away when I most wanted to embrace it. I believe it was my junior training to pass through those fires and get stronger. Starvation couldn't kill me, and rape failed to take my life. It seemed I had become invisible to death at a horrifying moment in life.

After two failed efforts, I gave up trying to die and started following my late mother's advice to pray to God for protection. I began to pray even in the warehouse. I preached the Gospel my mother had taught me, and I was no longer scared of those who could only kill my body. I began to fear Him who can destroy both the body and soul.

When I was about 14, I got pregnant for the first time, throwing up from morning sickness. My traffickers forced me to drink a concoction that caused an abortion. They forced three more abortions after that, and my constant question was, "God, are you really aware of all this?"

I had turned to God sincerely in my despair, but my faith was small. I had thoroughly rejected God when my mother died, and I tore up her beloved Bible page by page until it was empty. But when I realized I was powerless to take my life into my own hands, I clung to the shred of hope that my mother's words still offered me.

CHAPTER 5

Promoted

A trafficker's heart is at their back; they have no conscience or emotions. All they are interested in is money. My madam, Madam Malus the tigress, was once from a poor home. Her father was wealthy, while her mother was from an impoverished family. She grew up with deep hatred in her heart towards her father as she watched him mistreat and abuse her mother.

Despite everything her father did to her mother, no one arrested him for his crimes. Her mother's family forced her to remain with him until her father beat his wife to death one day. Madam Malus grew to hate men. In her quest for power and control, her spiritualist advised her to marry a husband and then sacrifice him by killing him. Madam Malus followed that advice without hesitation, and she became powerful and influential.

She didn't care who lived or died as long as the money continued to flow. She knew top politicians, and the police and army backed her up. If any of her workers or slaves were caught by the police for some act or another, Madam Malus only had to make one phone call to ensure their release.

If one of their trafficking victims escapes, people in her network will conspire to kill that person or return them to the madam. Traffickers are everywhere, including the churches. Some people have been initiated into the trafficking networks by a shrine ceremony or an oath to a deity. Others have been blackmailed into their role because the network has their nude videos. However, my madam mainly controlled her empire with witchcraft, so she didn't bother using video threats. She smuggles girls to Europe, selling them to traffickers, who pay her massive sums. Her network covers Malaysia, Turkey, Spain, Italy, Holland, and France. She used boys for drug trafficking, who would take drugs from Nigeria to South Africa, then from South Africa to another country.

What a terrible life Madam Malus leads. Sometimes when people say or preach, "Before you were born, God already knew what you would be," I must ask, did God know what kind of person my madam would become?

One night, I had a dream and saw a large bungalow house. I was inside with many children and their mothers while men with machine guns surrounded the house outside. At first, I tried first to poke my head out, but I heard gunshots and dodged the bullets. I ran inside, but I couldn't stay. I tried again to escape, and somehow, I managed to sneak quietly outside and made my way to another house, where I found a goldsmith.

He made protective armor for me and asked, "What will your armor be called?"

I replied, *"Ikuku ama n'onya,"* meaning, "Wind that can never be trapped."

The man put the armor on me, and I came out of the building.

When I woke up and realized it was a dream, it didn't make sense because I had no hope of escape or protection. I had only wished to be a wind that could never be trapped.

When I turned 16, I was "upgraded" from street beggar to full-time prostitution for political purposes. I was taken to a duplex brothel with other girls, where I served two clients daily. At least I was no longer a dirty person who had to beg on the streets, and I slept on a good mattress.

Once a girl's vagina no longer pleases Madam's clients, she often sends the unfortunate girl to corrupt policemen. They harvest and sell the girl's organs if Madam hasn't made the money she intended from that poor girl. To avoid this fate, we learned local ways of tightening the vagina, sometimes washing it with a particular concoction or even stitching it in more extreme cases. We also had to take something monthly to prevent us from getting pregnant.

After witnessing so much evil firsthand, I understand that life is not balanced. In Nigeria, the poor people envy the rich, but they have no idea of the dirty deals those people have done to achieve the life that the poor are envying.

The love of money is evil. We all were required to make a certain amount every month. If we made more than that amount, we still had to give the money to Madam. The only money we were allowed to keep was to buy clothes because we had to look good for the politicians. We had to pay a certain amount to Madam if we wanted to buy our freedom.

I was so young, still just a child, and learning about the evilest acts imaginable. Life is incredibly cheap to the traffickers, and some of my prostitute coworkers' deaths are indelibly stamped in my memory.

One girl, Joyce, was killed because she sent some money to her family without paying Madam for the month. They killed Martha for falling in love. These deaths were unmerited—their "offenses" did not deserve death.

I feel bad when I remember those poor girls, but at the time, I was happy for them and even jealous because I also wished to die. It seemed that only in death could I be free from this wicked world. It was a cruel, pathetic, and miserable life.

Now I understand that death is not truly the solution to most problems. I am alive and write to encourage you to take a bold step toward change and leave that self-bondage or self-brothel where you either put yourself or were forced into by others.

Living in the clutch of evil in Nigeria taught me a lot about the dark side of the world. There was no goodness, love, or peace. I experienced only hatred, anger, and torture.

Madam had seven brothels in our area in Nigeria. If you walked past one on the street, you wouldn't even know it was a brothel. Some of the brothels were places where men visited for sex, but we were usually sent away from my particular house to service men in other locations. Our house was located in a semi-busy area, with people buying and selling on the street beside us.

Madam gave me the freedom to go in and out of the house and even travel because I was spiritually controlled, not physically. I had been "broken in" behind locked doors in Ghana, but now I was free to move around because they knew I wouldn't run.

Most girls couldn't run away because they knew it would endanger their families. Once, one of the girls I knew didn't pay her money in time. Madam had her people find the girl's little sister and cut off her pinkie finger. They brought the severed finger and showed it to the girl.

Madam said, "If you don't pay, I will keep cutting all your little sister's fingers off."

And so we worked, standing on the street to bring men in. It was routine for me to be raped by three men at once. We worked all night and slept during the day. There were three girls in every room, but I wasn't friends with them. Madam didn't allow it, so I didn't talk to anyone but simply came back from the job and went to bed.

Sometimes, depending on the job I returned from, I couldn't sleep. When men gang-raped me, or two men raped me all night, I would come back and not be able to sleep. Sometimes I had no appetite because of what they had done in my mouth.

Madam would always tell me that these hard experiences would help my future. She wanted me to become strong and heartless, and she was succeeding. Under her guidance, I was becoming rude and mean. We couldn't just die; only torture or bleeding abortions would give us that privilege.

There was a little shop called Mama Pood where we bought hot, fresh food every day because we didn't cook. Life was only about survival, and there was no time to do anything but try to bring in the required money for the week. I couldn't even take care of myself if I didn't manage to make the target money.

At the time, we had a very evil head of house who controlled everything we did and often raped us at night. He told us that Madam was asking for 15,000 *naira* every week when she had only asked for 10,000 *naira* every week, and he kept the rest of the money. He beat me often; everyone beat me because I was a very stubborn girl.

Even though I was forced to work and give my earnings to Madam, I had never met her. I didn't know she had known about me before I was born or that she had a plan for me. She was breaking me in through this process, so I would become someone who would help her lead and do business.

She had a plan, but so did my Creator. They were at war to fulfill my destiny.

Who would win?

Madam was busy sending ladies abroad and men on business ventures, and I was learning about her kind of life. If one of her men failed her, they sold his kidneys. If a girl failed to please her clients and didn't have the money to pay off Madam, she would be killed mercilessly.

Life is not easy for the voiceless.

I learned about trafficking from the inside as one of the victims. Trafficking is when someone is used against their will to extract money from them. To achieve their aim, traffickers take their victims through many processes, including swearing oaths or threatening to publish naked pictures and videos of the trafficked victims on social media.

Trafficking is not only about women; it is about human beings. Although most victims are women or girls, men can be trafficked too. They follow traffickers to Dubai or other places, promised a high-paying job. But when they arrive at their destination, they are ordered to traffic drugs. If they try to refuse, the traffickers threaten their families. Some men are also trafficked for gay sex work or slave labor.

Even babies are sold, sometimes by evil people in hospitals who tell a poor young mother that her baby died from some invented disease. Sometimes I wonder what kind of planet this is, where such acts are carried out by guardians, parents, and family members. People have sold their own siblings to traffickers, just as Joseph's brothers did in the Bible. Such things still happen today, and many victims eventually commit suicide because of shame, torture, inflicted diseases, or health issues afterward.

My madam invested a lot of money into bribing people in power, and she didn't want that money to go to waste. She took her victims to a shrine so she could afterward control them with voodoo. My traffickers didn't brand me when I worked as a beggar, but they marked my body everywhere when I started regular sex work. I have a cross on my upper breast. They marked us everywhere on our private parts because they were used for our job. The marks came with a curse that if we tried to run away and be with a decent man, the curse would kill him.

Madam's victims were forced to swear an oath to a shrine, promising they would always behave well, respect their madam, and serve diligently. I preferred being killed by the oath to being killed by Madam's people, although I feared only the One who can kill the body and the soul, which is God, not just a man who can kill only the body. I rejected Madam and her control spiritually and physically, and these oaths have no influence or effect on me today. I am a new creature; old things have passed away.

CHAPTER 6

Head of House

After some time, Madam wanted to make me the head of house to be in charge of the brothel and manage the other ladies as we went out for our jobs. When my madam called with a place to send girls, I would arrange who would go. This position was less stressful because the head of house got to keep half the money they earned. I had to report everything to Madam, knowing that I might pay with my life if I covered anything up.

It was unusual for Madam to appoint one of the sex workers as head of house. Every other brothel had a man as head of house, but she liked me personally and fortified me to do the job. I took the lead, and the advantage was that I had a little break from performing so much sex work and could solicit for any of them. Though many sex workers were trafficking victims, some young ladies came to me as the head of house, asking to join us to earn money to support their families or pay their way through school.

Madam Malus came from America to Nigeria, and I was taken by one of her men to Abuja to meet her for increased voodoo fortification. Madam told me I needed higher fortification because of my promotion. She used a charm made from the blood of a little child. People in her organization ritually sacrifice babies, pounding them like other people pound pepper.

When I walked into the house where I had been taken, I saw a woman sitting in the salon like a guest.

She said, "How are you? You look very beautiful!"

I didn't know who she was, but she looked tiny and innocent. I was then invited into a chamber, and the guy with me locked the door behind us. Then the woman entered the room and changed into red and white spiritual attire.

She said, "I am Madam Malus."

That is when I knew she was my madam. She had summoned me there for ritual demonic abuse.

Madam had a private office with a big mirror. There were no books, the way there might be in a typical office. Instead of books, Madam studied us and how to control us spiritually. One of the things in her *covel*, or secret room, was the skin they took from our vaginas during the circumcision, used to control us. No one is allowed into that room unless Madam takes them there.

And now she had brought me into that room. Madam told me that she saw me as her own daughter, and I would take charge of her affairs after she died.

She put me in front of her second shrine and forced me to repeat after her, "If I ever betray you, I shall bleed to death."

As soon as I had said the oath, she cut me in the middle of my tongue with a razor. A python came out of the shrine and swallowed the razor. Madam then stripped naked, defecated onto a plate, made me eat it, then gave me red oil to wash my hands.

After that, she turned into a python and slithered into a traditional calabash voodoo pot. When she returned to her human form, she told me this was a sign that if I ever betrayed her or talked about her, I would die. Then she put a snake inside me and said that if I encountered a snake, I would know it was because of that snake she had placed in me. This was a spiritual experience, but I saw a physical snake.

You can imagine how terrified I was of snakes.

After that ritual, they took me to the forest, where only my madam and I entered, and we met the magician there. He and Madam took me to a shrine in an evil place and then put something in my vagina that put me into a trance for three days. On Monday, we sat on the forest floor, and they gave me two eggs and asked me to repeat after them. They cut my pubic hair and then asked me to lie down inside a casket. After that, I was spiritually fortified.

They opened the casket on Wednesday, after which they made all sorts of marks on my face, chest, back, and lower and upper vagina. Those marks were meant to protect me and not allow anyone to have sex with me without paying my madam. Only people approved by Madam could have sex with me— otherwise, either the other person or I would die.

Madam explained to me that she did all of this so I could advance in power and be prepared to inherit her empire when she died.

When I left the forest at the end of this process, I was taken to a tattoo shop and given a tattoo on my left arm to add more spiritual fortification. I don't know what it means, but it's a deeply embedded tattoo.

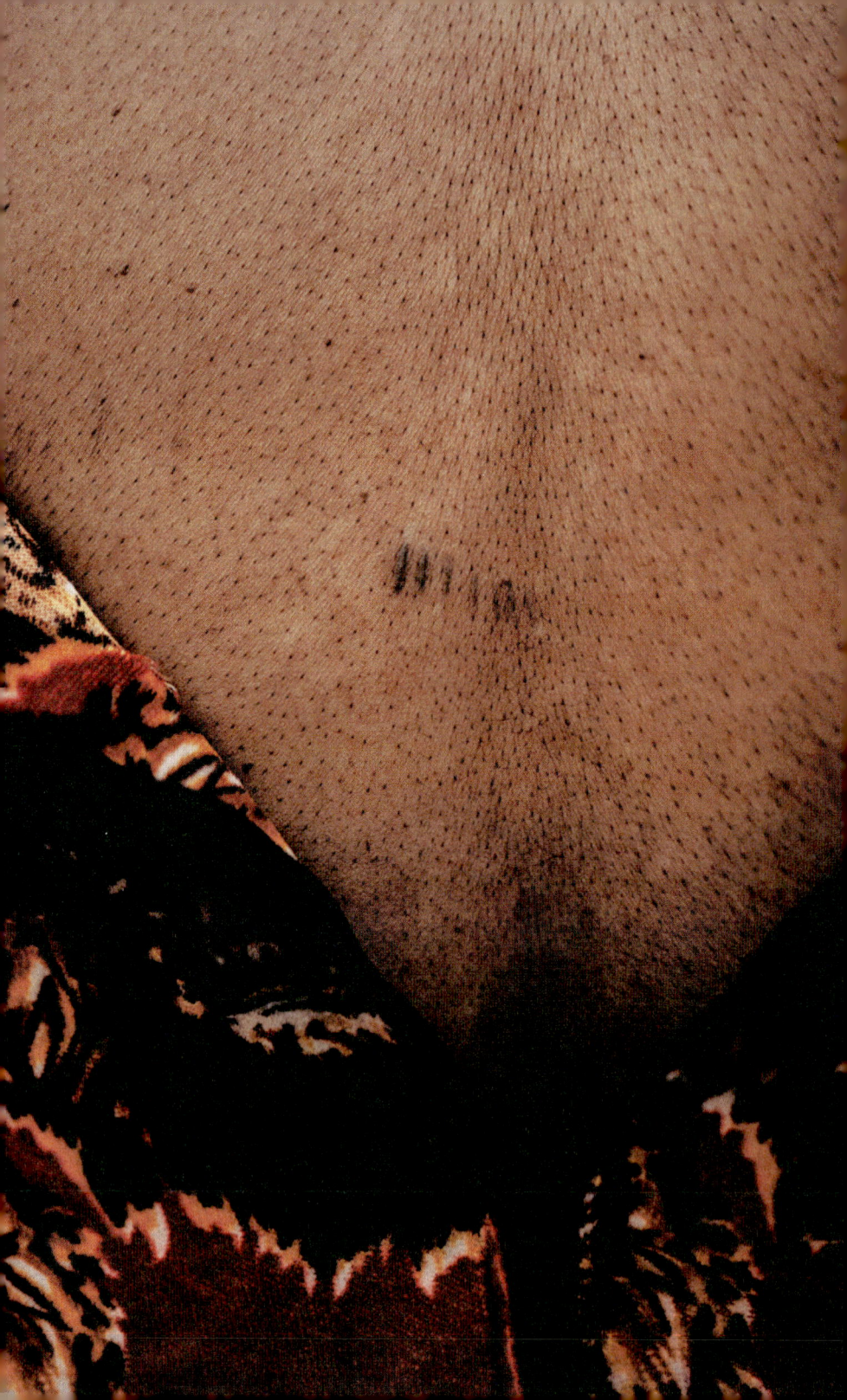

The higher you go in fortification, the more you can do spiritually.

After that, I stayed with Madam at her house in Abuja, and my clients were very wealthy men. Many of them were pastors. Some women came to the house to visit Madam Malus and had no idea who she really was. She was a very famous business-woman who sold gold as well as girls.

After a while, I traveled back to my city to continue working as the head of house. Madam sent me to a different brothel, and I met the four girls there. I felt good because I had been promoted and was given responsibility, even though I knew it was not a fun responsibility.

At first, the girls didn't like me because they felt I was too young to come and control them. They didn't respect me, so I met with the girls and invited workers from the other brothels. I told them they had to listen to me so they wouldn't have to face Madam. I explained that I was just like them before and that we all had to work together and help each other.

They liked the idea, and I started doing what I could to help them. If one was sick and couldn't work, I paid Madam the money they owed. The other heads of house would call me with jobs for the girls in my house. I rose to the challenge and tried to organize things to make the best life I could. As head of house, I had some terrible responsibilities like taking videos of the girls having sex and sending the videos to Madam Malus. Despite that, I tried to make their lives a little less severe.

After my promotion, I only served rich men, and torture and gang rapes were less common. I even started helping beggar children every Friday with the money I earned. They would line up at noon, and I distributed to each child a bag of rice with a small amount of cash inside.

I also went back to the first warehouse where I had lived to help the children I had been with. Because there were so many children, I could only remember the ones who had slept on my side of the bunk beds. I went to the warehouse to check on them and gave them money. Since I had been promoted by Madam, the men in the warehouse had to respect me now.

Because I knew what it was to be exploited, I was quick to understand people's situations. I was able to intervene and help some girls who owed fees and helped some mothers open a small business. I didn't want to see any vulnerable girl being exploited at all. I had to hustle even harder at sex work to pay my madam's regular money and still have enough to meet the needs of the people I was helping.

Madam made it clear that she wanted me to manage all the local affairs. Most of the other heads of houses reported to me. Since they knew I could easily have them killed, they respected me.

As head of house, many people come and ask you to sell the organs of the girls who are working for you. Some people will lie and tell their madam that a girl ran away, and then they sell the girl's organs for personal gain. I always told Madam when someone asked me this, and suddenly someone would disappear. Usually, they used a policeman who came and arrested the girl. While she was in his custody, her organs were harvested. They also used us for blood donations without our consent.

While working as head of house, I saw some women being used to birth a child. A man would pay to impregnate a girl, and when the child was born, the man would take the baby away. I thought of it as local IVF. The women screamed and cried when their babies were taken because they had not known that their child would be sold.

Other times, Madam would use the hospital to take a child. They would walk into the hospital, find the doctor who worked with Madam, and then give the baby and the placenta to the buyer. They would then tell the girl that her child had died. Most often, it was Madam herself that was doing this. I can't imagine a worse thing you could do to a woman than to take her child.

I feel guilty when I remember those poor mothers, but if we hadn't cooperated, they would have killed them on the spot. Surely it was better to at least save the mother's life. Seeing children taken from their mothers and the placenta being sold for some ritual was the second worst thing I endured as a trafficking victim.

My worst and most challenging job was being forced to do gruesome sexual acts. There is nothing you don't see in the prostitution field, especially when you're forced into it.

Deep down inside, I was sickened by it all, but I couldn't do anything about it. Poverty makes you handicapped and a victim of circumstances. I was powerless.

It is heartbreaking to think of a child being sold to another person without the mother's consent. Now that I am a mother who can't bear to be apart from her son, I cannot imagine him being taken away from me for a ritual, God forbid.

Night after night, my past still flashes before me with guilt and frustration. May God help the poor women who are still experiencing these things I've described. I pray they get genuine helpers, not someone like my madam, who claims to help you but takes away five things for every one she gives.

When I was head of house at the brothel, I felt positioned to help more people. Little did I know how much more was needed to provide real help. Many girls might have willingly entered the horrors of prostitution in search of food, education, or other benefits, but I managed to turn down most of the ones who asked to work for us and opted to instead help them with their most urgent needs.

I had to message or speak to Madam every day. If one of the girls was arrested, I had to call the police that worked with Madam to get her released.

When I became head of house, I changed a lot of things. I had nothing to lose. Sometimes I challenged madam, fighting about how much the girls had to pay her. Madam said one day, "You are as stubborn as your late mother. If your mother couldn't hide from me, what makes you think you can run away?"

From that statement, I concluded that my mother must have been trapped in Madam's organization, like me. Apparently, she had run away after I was conceived, though not far enough.

Those who work for Madam Malus cannot escape because she won't hesitate to kill their family members. Besides that, the oath they took will surely mess them up.

Madam controlled us from a voodoo mirror in her secret office. When she sent us on a dangerous job for political purposes, she would guide us with the mirror. She would speak to us through it, and we would hear her controlling us. Sometimes, she could even make the security personnel sleep when we walked past them.

One day, Madam summoned me back to Abuja, and she explained that since she wanted me to be respected, she would buy me a car. Madam gifted me a Jeep on my 18th birthday to meet with the politicians and businessmen in style. I was very happy. We had a large political party for my birthday, attended by many men, a few businesswomen, and even a former state governor.

One day, 12 of us girls were sent to a big celebration for a senator. I was in a Jeep with one other girl. The other 10 girls traveled by bus. The bus had a bad accident on the way, and six of the girls were killed while the other four were seriously wounded.

As I was driving, one of my tires flew off. I was driving recklessly fast on an express road. I braked hard, and the car behind me flipped over me in a somersault. The tire from my car was rolling around like someone was chasing it.

One of the other head of house personnel called the girl with me and asked, "Did Sarah die? If she dies, just wave new money in her face, and she will sneeze and come back to life."

I was seriously attached to money, so they used to say that money would wake me from the dead.

Some people passing by on the road stopped and helped me. I sent the car to be fixed and took a taxi home without a scratch.

If there was any politician or businessman more powerful than Madam, she would send one of us girls to help her get rid of him. They would set up a meeting with the man, and the girl would go to a hotel to meet him. The man would bring drinks.

We would have our nails done long before such an assignment, and Madam would put poison powder in our bras. We would smoothly get a little poison under our long nail before picking up the man's cup to taste it while simultaneously dipping the poisoned nail into his drink.

I was sent on such a mission to a very evil man. When he took his cup, his hand started shaking. He asked me, "What did you put into the glass?"

At the same time, I heard Madam call, "Sarah! Sarah!" and the man grabbed me. I broke free from him, ran out of the hotel, and escaped.

As head of house, I serviced only businessmen and politicians. Some of them didn't even want sex; they just wanted company. They liked that I talked a lot, and I even gave them ideas for their business.

Sometimes I preached to them and asked, "If you die on top of me now, where do you think you're going?"

One man said he had never thought of that before, and he stopped having sex. I told him he should focus on growing his business since he was a rich man, and I gave him a great idea for importing. This man would sometimes give me money for nothing, and like this, I was able to help people. That man wanted to take me away from Madam, but I knew I could never go.

One day, Madam gave us a job. I traveled to another city, went to the appointed place, and waited for the client but didn't see him. The client we went to see didn't come, but other politicians came, one being a speaker of the house of assembly. These were very wealthy people. Another wanted girls to sacrifice for money. He told me I was too innocent to be killed, but I felt he might kill me.

I was in the hotel reception with three girls and saw a leader of one of the tribes in Nigeria with a briefcase. I had the feeling this man was wealthy, so I went to meet him. I told him I was waiting for a client who hadn't shown up, and I needed money now because I had to make 300,000 *naira* (Madam had sent me for 200,000 *naira*). This man gave me 1 million *naira* in cash and told me to take my 300,000 and give the other three girls the rest. I gave the girls their share and told them to go.

The man looked evil, but I needed to pay him back, so I accompanied him to his room. When we got inside, he went into the shower. I took the chance to open his briefcase, and a live python came out of the bag.

I screamed and said, "Please don't kill me! I am a motherless child! I have people I am trying to save!" In my terror, I passed out.

That was around 9:00 p.m., and I didn't wake up until about 2:00 a.m., lying across the bed. I saw the man doing something on his laptop, and I started yelling that his briefcase was evil.

He said, "Don't steal, even to help others. Don't you know that you shouldn't touch everything you see? This briefcase is the source of my power."

As if I wasn't frightened enough already, he said, "You're the first person I didn't kill when they messed with my power."

He then called a taxi and gave me money for the trip. Before I left, he opened his towel and exposed himself to me, and I saw a snake where his private parts should have been. It was still dark when I left and went to the airport to fly back to my city.

Another time, I took two girls to a job in another city. We arrived at the hotel where we had been sent, and the people there separated me from the other two girls. I could see the window of the room where the girls had been taken, and I heard screams coming from there. As I looked at the window, a body came flying out of it and fell past me. I told the man I was with that I needed to go and order something. When I ran down to the first floor and outside, I saw one of the girls lying dead in the street. I ran from the hotel and never saw those girls again.

There is nothing too extreme in that world. One man working for Madam was required to have sex with a dead girl to use the sperm to fortify a politician.

Being held in the grip of Nigerian evil is to experience hell on earth.

CHAPTER 7

The Persistent Pastor

Since our madam controlled us through spiritual force, only a greater spiritual power could threaten her. For this reason, Madam Malus was worried about pastors coming into our area. To reduce the threat they posed, we would post pornographic material on the street of one of us and a pastor in bed. Sadly, some pastors also attacked other pastors by doing the same thing to blackmail them. If we failed to seduce a pastor to get these videos and pictures, we would use another method. I would go to the pastor's office with a camera hidden in a hair clip or car key. In the office, I would remove my clothes and take the most sexually suggestive picture I could, and then use the photo to create a scandal.

Since the white men brought materialistic Christianity to African countries, we are now enslaved to a false mentality. We rarely see examples of true Christianity. To find authentic followers of Jesus, you must get outside the shell of Christianity in Nigeria, which is a business in reality.

Many Nigerian streets have multiple churches on them. You'll find Nigerian church names for every letter of the alphabet. The Bible says many are called, but few are chosen, and I see that among the men who call themselves pastors. Gullible followers fall for the tricks and miracles performed by these men. Some "healers" even pay people to pretend to have an affliction and then claim to be healed when the pastor touches them.

I know of pastors who fly on private jets and travel abroad when needing medical care. Meanwhile, they give their members some holy water, holy stickers, or a holy handkerchief when they are sick. Pastors preach that God protects us, but they have bodyguards and military men to protect them. They ask their members to contribute money to build church-run schools, but those same donors can't afford to send their children to the school because it's too expensive.

Churches advertise themselves like a market or store: "Come to our church where God is doing miracles!" Yet people of different churches cannot worship together. No wonder many Nigerians are convinced that Christianity is a scam.

Many pastors would come to the brothel and yell at us to repent of our wickedness, saying, "Repent, for the kingdom of God is here."

I would reply, "Get out! Where is the kingdom of God?"

I was very cynical about pastors and churches because I thought they were all hypocritical and judgmental. If you're a woman and you smoke, they automatically label you a prostitute. If you wear a mini skirt in public, you will be followed by men who think you are available. If such ordinary actions cause women to be called prostitutes, how judgmental do you think they are toward real prostitutes?

A woman who has been in a brothel, whether voluntarily or not, can seldom expect to get married. The church will be the first to reject and discredit such a woman and her family. Even the mother of a prostitute will be excommunicated for her daughter's sins. Abortion seems to be the only option in Nigeria because the child of a prostitute will not be accepted or adopted.

If an unmarried girl gets pregnant, she will be cast out of the church. The shaming and rejection are meant to dissuade women from fornication but often result in secret abortions. If a prostitute visits a Nigerian church, she'll probably have to sit in what is called the "back chair." It's like the seat of shame.

I would only go to church when I was invited for special events like a baby dedication. I recognized the pastor as one of my clients on one such occasion.

The people in the church were testifying about the pastor, "This pastor prayed for me, and now I conceived, and my affliction left me."

I was tempted to go up to the podium and say, "Praise the Lord, church. I am a prostitute, and your pastor is one of my clients. Isn't that a miracle?"

But then I thought, *I don't want to destroy the faith of these people. I'll just let them be their stupid selves.*

The next time I saw that pastor as my client, I asked him what he would have done if I had testified against him. I told him the only reason I hadn't exposed him was that I didn't want people to lose faith in God as I had.

One of the women I had helped financially invited me to her church one day. As soon as I stepped through the door, I broke out in goosebumps all over my body. At first, I thought all the voodoo markings on my body were reacting to a holy place, but that didn't make sense, so I said I had an emergency and needed to leave. When I told Madam, she informed me that the pastor had buried a live cow in the front of the church in a ritual to attract members and fake miracles.

When I learned that he counseled people on Wednesdays, I paid the 1,000 *naira* he charged for a meeting and went to see him.

He took my money before asking, "What problem do you need help with? Be quick, as I have a lot of other clients to see."

"I am here to blackmail you," I retorted confidently. "You need to pay me for my silence because you're a disgrace to the title of pastor and to God."

"I rebuke you, you foul spirit," he declared before beginning to blabber in some unknown tongue.

"Be quiet," I said. Then I reminded the pastor of everything I knew about him and his secret life. I told him he was just wasting my time, and I made him pay me to keep quiet.

That same night, that idiot pastor called me and paid for sex.

Some people practiced voodoo, and I could accept them, but I couldn't stand pastors who tried to mix voodoo and Christianity. I hated that nonsense.

One Nigerian pastor truly wanted to help the girls in the brothels. He would find the prostitutes on the streets and tell them, "I want to help you get away from here."

When a girl was brave enough to leave and start a new life, this pastor would help her find housing and get job training. He understood the financial difficulty of starting with nothing and supported the former prostitutes practically. He even helped some girls find husbands and paid for their weddings. This is the kind of practical help these women need.

I never saw anyone come inside Madam's brothels to try to help the girls because she would have killed them. Everyone knew better than to enter her territory.

If a pastor came and tried to preach to us from the street, one of the girls would tell me that my boyfriend was outside. I would then go out and try to seduce the pastor. However, one refused to give in to me and kept coming back to preach to us.

He would come straight below my window and yell, "Sarah, the kingdom of heaven is at hand. You must repent."

"What did I do to you," I yelled back.

If I wasn't at the window, he would go get a Coca-Cola and wait, and then he would continue calling to me persistently.

Finally, Madam Malus ordered us to rape him, so three of us girls attacked him and raped him so he wouldn't come back.

Madam Malus told me that anything that distracted me was an enemy to my success. Since the pastors were a distraction, they were my enemies. Despite her justifications, I am deeply ashamed of my part in attacking that good man. I still hold a deep grudge against myself for it.

That same pastor came back and invited us to church. I was shocked to see that he was not ashamed to return after what we had done to him.

"You again!" I said. "Are you not ashamed?!"

"You can hurt my body, but you cannot hurt my spirit," he said.

One of the girls said we need to deal with this guy once and for all, but I asked her, "Are you sure this is not God Himself tormenting us?"

Despite our attack on him, he was not afraid of us—in fact, I was the scared one. All the other pastors gave up when we chased them off, but never this man.

He told me, "You can use your beauty to glorify God."

This persistent pastor kept coming to the gate, knocking and requesting me by name. At last, I decided to visit his church with two other girls.

The pastor welcomed us and said, "Jesus loves you no matter what you have done. If you feel guilty, come and we will talk to God."

The other two girls accepted his invitation, and he urged them to repent and ask God for forgiveness. He told the girls to inform me that he wanted to see me since I was in charge, to urge me to set an example for the girls under my care by turning to God in repentance. When I heard he wanted to see me, I assumed he was like the other pastors I knew and just wanted to have sex, so I didn't go.

However, I was wrong about him. Unlike the others, he was a good pastor.

Other pastors who came and shouted at us were harsh, unloving, and judgmental. When I heard one of them yelling from the street, I opened the brothel door and poured water on his head.

"Are you mad?" I asked.

"I cast you out! I bind you!" the man yelled.

"Go bind your own family!" I shouted back.

Some of the pastors shouted their condemnation as early as 6 a.m. We would return from doing a job at 5 a.m., and the preaching would start an hour later.

That pastor we raped kept coming back, not shouting condemnation like the others, but expressing sincere concern for us.

I dreamed one night that all of us in the brothel were tied up and getting beaten. I connected it to this persistent pastor and told the other girls that he was a real man of God.

When he came back again, I told him about my dream. He said it was not a person punishing us in what I saw, but the Holy Spirit, since our actions were a sin against Him. He encouraged us to kneel with him, and when we did, he prayed and asked Christ to forgive us because we didn't know what we were doing.

Then he said, "Since you don't want to attack me any longer, can I preach to you again? Christ is love, no matter what you have done."

The pastor gave me his number and told me I could call him anytime if I needed help. "You have a good spirit," he said. "Why are you doing this kind of work?"

"It's just a business," I told him. "Why don't you forget about the ones you'll never convert? You know I can't be forgiven after what I did to you. How can I repent?"

He said, "I want to preach to YOU, Sarah. I can preach to the other girls, but they will be pulled back because of you and your influence. You won't repent because you are afraid of the one who will kill the body, but you are more than a body. You have a heart! You have a soul! There is someone inside you."

As strange as it seems, the persistent pastor became our friend. He came every weekend and preached the love of Jesus for us. Even though we were friendly, he never ate or drank anything because he was afraid we would drug him. He was the only pastor we ever let into the brothel.

The other pastors continued to get water dumped on them. Once, I even put hot pepper in the water and yelled at one of them to get his attention. I poured the water into his face as he looked up, hoping the pepper would burn his eyes.

I was trained to hate pastors, but the persistent one was different.

One day he even said, "Someday, you will preach the Gospel more than me."

We laughed cynically at him, and I asked, "Are you looking for preaching candidates?"

But despite our mockery, I genuinely trusted this man. I would leave whatever I was doing to listen to him when he came. One day, I even ended my phone call with Madam when I heard his voice at the door. I told her I needed to use the bathroom as an excuse to go talk to him.

I really hurt that pastor. Of everything wrong I have done, this is the most shameful one to me.

Madam Malus thought pastors could convert us and change our destiny, and she was determined that I would take the path she had chosen for me. She forced us to be like her, but the person my mother had trained me to be was still alive somewhere deep inside me. I was still helping people in need, and I never betrayed my pastor friend to Madam.

One day the pastor came, and I was furious because one of the girls had stolen from a client and would be killed for the theft. He asked why I was so upset, and I explained that one of the girls would be killed for stealing.

"Sarah, are you serious?" he gasped. "Have you created life before? Then how can you want to take a life?"

He preached so compellingly to me that he convinced me not to tell Madam about the girl's theft. He said that since Jesus had stood in my place, I could stand in that poor girl's place and protect her.

I would have reported the theft to Madam Malus because I thought I didn't have a choice. But when the pastor persuaded me otherwise, I trusted him enough to do what he said.

His intervention saved that girl's life. She had been crying and packing her bags, knowing that a policeman was coming to get her. The officer would oversee her killing and the harvesting of her organs. She was aware of the penalty for stealing from clients, so she knew exactly what to expect. I realized that I had a choice after the pastor convinced me to save her, and I always covered for the girls after that.

I was so fascinated by this pastor that, one day, I decided to try to live like him and preach on the street. After the horrible thing we did to him, he still loved us and spoke life to me. He told me he saw me in his dreams and said I was destined to preach the Gospel.

So one day, I took my microphone out into the street and preached, "Repent for the kingdom of heaven is at hand!" I did this for several hours, and I felt so happy. But when I finished, I felt ashamed of myself. What would my fellow prostitutes say when they heard?

Someone on the street saw me preaching and called the girls in the house to ask them if I was there.

"Someone who looks like Sarah is preaching on the street!" they exclaimed.

When I returned to the brothel, the other girls asked me, "Did you drink last night? Are you drunk?"

My preaching shocked the girls because I was such a good worker for Madam, which meant doing many wicked things to make money, and here I was, out on the street, preaching. One of the girls from the brothel called Madam and told her I had been preaching.

She called me and said, "So you want to open a church? Go ahead, and the girls that attend it can work for us."

I had to pay Madam 500,000 *naira* for punishment. She declared that the pastor must have cursed me since I acted so strangely. Her greatest disappointment was that my spiritual fortification didn't seem to be working. After all of the rituals she did, the pastor's spiritual power was not supposed to affect me.

"How can a pastor control you?" she demanded. "What kind of power does he have?"

"It's time for you to repent as well!" I told her boldly.

She said, "If that pastor comes near me, I will drag him in and rape the Spirit of God right out of him."

Madam suspected that I was dating the pastor, which made her deeply suspicious. If there is one threat that will take a girl out of the brothel, it is a boyfriend.

But that pastor kept looking for me every time he came, never failing to remind me that God loved me. I was caught between the powerful reality he taught and the power of evil that controlled me. Most of me resonated with everything he said.

The girls started telling me that Madam wanted to kill my pastor friend. I knew it was not an idle threat since she had a hitman named Imeh who killed people for her.

I called and warned the pastor that Madam was plotting his death, but he just said, "She can kill my body, but she can't kill my soul."

He was a courageous and stubborn young man. Since he had very little money, I gave him some and urged him to use it to flee the country.

"Stop going to brothels to preach," I begged him. "The madams are very dangerous."

He replied, "You cannot stop me from preaching."

I never saw him again, but I tried to live out what he had taught me.

CHAPTER 8

Travel

One day I was summoned again to Madam's house in Abuja. She had a big job she wanted me to do, and she had called her spiritualist to do special fortification rites for me.

Madam hired her spiritual director, a voodoo high priest who advised and guided her spiritually. She relied on this man and his ability to predict the future. Madam could provide him in return with the human parts he needed for sacrifices because of her position. They were the perfect partners in crime.

On this occasion, Madam Malus was warned by the spiritualist that I would be her downfall. Others scoffed at the idea, asking, "How can a small rat like Sarah be the downfall of Madam Malus?"

However, the spiritualist insisted that I posed a threat and advised Madam to kill me or dismiss me from her service. The other head of house was also speaking against me, telling Madam that I was a problem and didn't like them. This person didn't work at all, and they made the girls work extra hard for personal gain. I was angry with them, and that's why they reported me.

My madam's spiritualist continued to caution her that I would be her undoing and that she needed to move me out of Africa if she wanted to keep me. At one point, he asked me to leave the room, and upon my return, Madam looked me up and down with disdain. "How can this baby threaten me?" she demanded.

The spiritualist said, "Have you ever seen a dragon give birth to a baby dragon?"

"How can Sarah threaten me?" Madam persisted. "Her mother could not run from me."

Madam had taken me when I was young, so she had a lot of control over me. However, she didn't realize that God knew all about me before I was ever born.

Madam told me that the spiritualist advised her, "I see Sarah being a threat to you in the future."

The priest then fortified me for the job I was summoned for by cutting me and rubbing powder into the cuts. They then sent me to take down a pastor who was doing many miracles.

After that counsel from her guide, Madam told me I would be leaving Nigeria. I was eager to travel, and my biggest wish was to go to America. She told me I had a job to do in Europe first, and after that, she would take me to America.

Madam began the process of preparing for my travels. She got me a passport and took me to two different European embassies, but they rejected my applications.

The spiritualist again urged Madam to kill me, but she refused, although she warned me that I was getting out of hand. I knew that any threat she made was not to be taken lightly. After a girl had undergone the circumcision initiation with the witch doctor, Madam could see everything the individual said and did in her mirror. Of course, this ability gave her considerable control over the girls.

One of the girls in the brothel had been jealous of me. She had been in the house before I arrived, and she was angry that I had been appointed head of house. When Madam saw this girl being mean to me, she cursed her. The girl died with blood running from her mouth.

I was upset by the killing, but when I talked to Madam about it, she said, "You don't know how many people I killed because of you."

That was the first time I realized Madam Barine had been killed because of me.

I honestly believe the spiritualist saw the future because I have faith that I am a threat to Madam, and that I am meant to stop the majority of the trafficking in Nigeria. I will bring her down if she stands in my way because all power belongs to Jesus Christ. No weapon formed against me shall prosper, and He that is in me now is greater than any Madam or the prince of this world.

When I accepted Christ, I got baptized and became a new creation. Old things have passed away, and all things have become new. Therefore, no evil shall befall me and my household. God has given the angels charge over me to keep me in all my ways.

Madam tried to elevate my prostitution to an international level by sending me to Europe, but I was rejected because those were not the destinations chosen by God for me. God's purpose for me would be manifested in a different place entirely.

After my applications for Europe were rejected, Madam next tried Turkey, and my visa application was accepted. Three other girls, happy to be leaving Nigeria because they thought they might have an opportunity to run away in a new land, traveled with me. They didn't mind dying because of the life we were living.

Two men and a girl met us at the airport in Turkey, confiscating our passports before taking us to a basement apartment, where we slept. A taxi would take us to a hotel where we serviced the men.

Many of the Turkish clients were particularly evil. They forced us to take drugs, and one of them tried to dehumanize me by making me eat his feces. If I had still been head of house, I would not have allowed such things to happen on my watch.

Madam had one particular job she wanted me to do in Turkey. I was supposed to get information from a man, and I used the drug Madam had provided for the task. When the man was unconscious, I removed a flash drive from his wallet as instructed.

I was angry at Madam because she left me to the mistreatment of Turkish men who subjected me to some of the worst experiences in my life. Here, I didn't know my clients. I simply went wherever I was ordered and did what I had to. I had no part in making the deals—we just had to satisfy the men, no matter how many.

Madam told me that I had a choice to pay her $50,000 for my freedom, or I could serve her diligently for 10 years. She knew I was stuck. At this point, I became weak in body and soul, sleeping with all kinds of different men. Nothing about it was easy.

One day I had a dream where I saw an HIV-positive man. Later, when I walked into a client's room, I recognized the man from my dream. He wanted to have unprotected sex, but I refused.

He insisted, "I paid for unprotected sex!"

Remembering the dream, I somehow found the courage to resist, so I ran out of the room and went to the elevator. It was usually busy, but the elevator was on the right floor this time. The door immediately opened when I pushed the button, and I escaped my predicament for the moment.

But when I got back to the apartment, Madam called and instructed the staff to punish and torture me. First, they locked me outside in the cold, and then they beat me mercilessly.

I tried to protest, telling them that I was a head of house in Nigeria.

"You aren't one abroad," they said, continuing to beat me.

As they flogged me, I quoted to my tormentors something from the Bible that I remembered: "Even if worms feed on my skin, this I know, that my Redeemer lives.

"You're talking rubbish," one of them said. "I heard you were stubborn, but this is Turkey."

I sustained many injuries from that merciless beating.

I was locked outside the house for hours. Even though I suffered from exposure to the cold, it afforded me a short reprieve from prostitution. It was the beginning of God helping me toward a safer place and an escape from my suffering.

When I was locked out of the house, a man approached me and asked, "Why are you in the cold?" He was a Nigerian drug trafficker, and he took me to his apartment and had sex with me.

You aren't afraid of falling when you're flat on the floor already. There was not much evil that I could be afraid of anymore.

After three days, Madam's people let me back into the house and gave me another job.

When I was in the brothels, we were not allowed to wear clothes at night. They wanted to make it easy to rape us, and if we were caught wearing clothes, they would be removed and tied around our necks. Because of the warm climate in Nigeria, being forced to sleep nude was not a hardship, but the Turkish winter made it miserable. Although the apartment had heat, it was still chilly, but we couldn't sleep with clothes on.

I had already tried to end my life by drinking kerosene and jumping into a well, yet here I was. Death refused me when I sought it, but it took my mother, who wasn't yet ready.

CHAPTER 9

Turkish Hell

Some mornings, I woke up vomiting and feeling weak. Whenever that happened, I would be given a pregnancy test. This happened roughly every three months. When the test was positive, I would be forced by my traffickers to have an abortion with a vaginal tablet or sent to the hospital where an abortion would be performed. One pregnancy wasn't caught as early as usual, and I was four months along before they aborted it. I saw the baby after this abortion, and it was already formed.

Before I came to Turkey, I had endured about 18 abortions, so Madam finally provided me with a morning dose of herbal medicine to stop menstruation. By the time I was in Turkey, I was no longer menstruating.

Janet was one of the girls who had traveled to Turkey with me. One day she said, "Listen, guys, we are abroad now. Maybe Madam's voodoo only works in Africa. Let's run away. Police here are not biased; they protect people and will help us."

Her arguments persuaded us, and we agreed to escape together. However, as we were sneaking away from the premises, something felt wrong. I changed my mind and said I couldn't leave after all. Janet was still eager and determined, but I felt my strength fade into weakness.

I said, "No, I am going back."

Sandra followed me, and Janet left.

That same evening, the doorbell rang, and we saw some policemen at the door. I felt a momentary surge of relief as I assumed that Janet had reported our captivity to the Turkish police, who were now coming to rescue us. But my heart sank as I saw the police had Janet handcuffed as they said, *"Tamam! Tamam!"* which I understood as saying that she was finished.

The officers handed Janet over to the head of house. The staff took Janet to the bathroom, tied her hands behind her back, and made the rest of us girls watch as they drowned her in the bathtub.

"I hope you all saw what happened to her," the head of house told us curtly.

I thought only the Nigerian government was corrupt, but this showed me that corruption could be anywhere.

I asked someone for advice about escaping from Turkey, and I was told to go to the police for help. This person explained that the police would deport me back to Nigeria. I wasn't interested in returning to my homeland, as that would have been a suicide mission. Madam's people would soon track me down, kill me, and harvest my organs.

While I was in Turkey, some very dark blood came out of my body. Since it was only a minuscule amount, I didn't worry about it at first. In the meantime, I was still dreaming of freedom and safety. After seeing what happened to Janet, I knew it would take a miracle to escape, but I was praying earnestly for just such a miracle.

Then one morning I started feeling sick again. I had a positive pregnancy test and realized I was pregnant by the Nigerian man who took me in from the cold and had unprotected sex with me.

My pregnancy led to a dispute between the father of my child and Madam Malus's agents. I was seasoned in evil, so I knew he was an evil man. I had only gone with him because I was freezing in the street and needed somewhere to stay. Now they were fighting about whether he would pay the balance to buy me from my madam, they would abort my child, or they would let me give birth and sell the baby. Despite all the abortions I had been forced to have, I didn't want this child to be aborted, nor was I willing to let him be sold.

It was an act of God that I conceived again because I hadn't even had a period for eight months due to the herbal concoction we took. When I learned I was pregnant, I didn't understand how it could have happened, but I did remember the light blood flow a little earlier.

I was given the prescribed concoction to end the pregnancy, but nothing happened. Next, the staff inserted a tablet through my vagina and made me swallow two more pills, but still, nothing happened. They summoned the home service doctor to do the abortion at home. After examining me, the doctor said because I was already so far along, he couldn't perform the abortion there unless they wanted me to die.

Madam ordered her staff to take me to the hospital, but I refused to go. They chained both hands above my head and tortured me with water and electric shocks. They even tried to reach into my body and pull the baby out. When that didn't work, four men took turns raping me until I bled. Finally, they heated a knife and made a cut on my stomach, telling me they were going to perform the abortion themselves.

I had believed my many forced abortions had damaged my womb beyond repair, so I wanted to escape and save this baby. A deep passion settled into my heart to protect my child, who could not be killed by the usual methods.

I passed out, and while I was unconscious, I dreamed that I was running while carrying a tiny baby boy on my shoulder. That dream motivated me to run, but I had no idea how to do it.

When I regained consciousness, the doctor said I was still pregnant. I knew the next attempt would be ten times worse than all I had endured to that point, so I agreed to go to the hospital with the doctor and the head of house.

The head of house had to wait in the reception area, and I followed the doctor, still determined to save my baby but feeling broken and helpless. On our way to the operating room for the abortion, I saw a sign that said EXIT. A man was guarding the door we had entered, so I knew I couldn't escape that way. However, this sign indicated a different exit door, and I felt a sudden surge of hope that I might be able to run away from here.

I told the doctor I needed to pee, so she showed me to the toilet and told me to come to her office afterward. The head of house was stationed to watch me in the hallway. I went into the bathroom and waited a bit, and when I looked outside the door, the man wasn't watching anymore. I exited through the door I had seen and ran barefoot into the market.

CHAPTER 10

Barefoot Escape

I ran into a market in Aksaray, Turkey and saw many Africans from Uganda, Cameroon, Congo, Nigeria, and Senegal. Something in my spirit led me to approach a very tall man and ask for help. I told him I was being pursued by people who wanted to kill me.

The man quickly took me to an African restaurant where I tried to avoid detection in a dimly lit area. After seeing some men eyeing me suspiciously in the restaurant, he moved me to another place. The men knew something was up because I was barefoot and unkempt. He quickly took me out of there to avoid further attention, and we went straight to a place like an agent's office.

My rescuer urged me to go to the police and make a report, but I refused, remembering how the police had returned Janet to be killed by Madam Malus's staff. Besides, my traffickers had my passport, so I would be deported back to Nigeria and into the deadly clutches of my madam. Escaping her is never easy, and as far as I know, I am the only person to survive running away from her in Turkey.

The man suggested that, without my passport, the only option was to cross from Turkey to Europe by sea as many refugees were doing. I preferred to die in the water than return to captivity, so I didn't hesitate to agree.

When I asked my rescuer why he was helping me, he said, "Many years ago, before I became a man and traveled abroad, someone came to my home and took my sister abroad to work. She never returned, and she has not called us or sent any message to my family. If she's still alive, I hope someone will help her as I'm helping you."

Many parents, believing that their child will have a good job in another country, willingly let their children go. The poor parents have no idea that they willingly sent their children to be trafficked.

Oh God, help the captives to be free.

When a poor family with many children is offered an opportunity to send a child abroad, they often agree without thoroughly investigating. This has led to the trafficking and deaths of many, many children.

My rescuer took me to Izmir on the west coast of Turkey, just a short way across the Aegean Sea from Europe. That man was undeniably sent by God to help me reach the destination determined for me. God wanted me to experience His goodness and to testify that, in every situation, we can give thanks and praise because He has a perfect plan. I pray that the young man who helped me will one day be reunited with his sister again.

When we reached Izmir, my guide arranged for the smugglers to take me to Europe. He even gave me money for food, and I spent four days in a guest house with other people waiting to go to Europe. One day, the police came to the guest house and took away anyone who didn't have an ID. I had no ID, but no one asked me anything. I was sitting on the staircase, with so much in my head. I was bleeding and thinking about how to save the life of my unborn child. I believe God blinded their eyes. I stayed there and waited until the smuggler came, and when he arrived with some other people, he said we were leaving that night.

Six adults and four children squeezed into one taxi for the trip to the seaside. I no longer cared whether I survived the trip or what happened to me because I was sure any outcome was better than going back to the life I had escaped. We got to a place at one point where the car couldn't continue, so we had to walk. When we saw a police patrol coming, the smugglers told us to lie low in a gutter. Miraculously, none of the babies cried, and the police passed by without detecting us.

I prayed, "God, my life is a testimony. Satan will seem to have won if I die here, and you are a jealous God. Will you allow me to perish here in hunger and starvation?"

We stayed in the forest that day with no food, water, or shower. Although I was already two months pregnant, God, in His infinite mercy, kept me healthy and strong while hiding in the forest.

I saw groups of Syrian refugees walking down to the seaside, speaking a language I didn't understand. Some people were pumping up an inflatable raft, and refugees began scrambling into the boat as soon as it was ready. Everyone, from old people to parents to children to babies, was getting in as fast as possible.

For the first time in my life, I was at liberty to choose my destiny. I could either ride this boat to an unknown destination or return to the living hell of a sex slave in Turkey. I boarded the vessel, quickly jumping into the raft with more than 50 others. Nobody asked me for money, which was a mercy from God, as I didn't have any. It was just me and my pregnancy—no siblings, no parents, no friends.

While crossing the water, I couldn't think about anything except reaching a safe place to deliver this child who refused to die after all the torture and medications designed to kill him. My body felt frail and exhausted, but I was determined to live long enough to give birth to this child. Nothing but his safety mattered to me.

The sea wasn't terrifying to me because all death is death. I had survived too many waves and storms to be afraid of a drop of rain. Whether you die on the land, in the sea, or in the air, death is ultimately the same.

In the middle of the sea, the balloon boat began bobbing wildly as the waves increased, and people were crying out in fear. The Christians shouted for Jesus to save them, while the Muslims made the same plea to Allah.

I felt sorry for all the frightened children on the boat, but I was indifferent to the danger we were in. If the boat capsized, I preferred death in the salty water to the fate that awaited me if I fell back into Madam's clutches.

Suddenly, I saw a boat coming toward us across the rough water. It bore a flag that was neither Nigerian nor Turkish, and I breathed a deep sigh of relief when I saw that it was a European vessel. The volunteers on the boat welcomed us aboard, gave us blankets, and cared for us.

They told us, "Don't worry, you're safe now. We're not from Turkey, so we won't take you back there."

At first, I expected to be raped, as it usually happened when I was in a vulnerable place, but to my great surprise, this rescue was for real. No more rapes, no more beatings, and no more imprisonment by Madam and her henchmen.

When we reached the European coast, I had no idea where in the world I was. I was just happy because I was no longer in Turkey, a country of torture and abuse for me.

The police and the volunteers who intercepted us took us to an isolated temporary camp since it was the weekend. Later, they moved us to another camp near one of the larger towns on the island. This camp was one of the largest camps housing the refugees who made the crossing from Turkey. I arrived at the camp on November 11, 2017.

The rescue team told me, "Don't be afraid; you are safe here in Europe."

That's when I understood where I was. I was being treated like a woman, or should I say, as a human being, for the first time since I was 12 years old.

My years of slavery and endless pain were over at last. I read in the Bible that weeping may endure for a night, but joy comes in the morning. My morning had arrived, my joy had come, and the grace of God had started speaking to me. I am a conqueror and a survivor. I am what God said I will be because I believe in the plan of God for my life. No man speaks in my life what God has not spoken.

My destiny lay outside my home country of Nigeria, but how could an orphan girl possibly travel abroad? The Bible says that Joseph also had a purpose in a foreign land. God allowed

Joseph to be trafficked and sold to get him there, so that purpose could be fulfilled. Similarly, I was also trafficked and sold before I reached the point where my destiny decreed I should be.

Someday, the purpose of God in my life will be manifest when I carry out my destiny and begin an organization, which will be called MTRH. This stands for Mother Tina Rehabilitation Home, named in honor of my Mother. And by God's grace, child trafficking will be reduced or stopped.

Painting Inspired by Monique's Story

CHAPTER 11

Fight for Life

I was 11 weeks pregnant and bleeding when I arrived in Europe in November 2017. The volunteers provided us with blankets and took our names. I slept inside a big tent with other women. One obviously pregnant lady was taken to Section C, where expectant mothers were housed. Since my pregnancy wasn't showing very much, no one realized I was pregnant, and I was still bleeding.

I kept to myself in the packed tent, not speaking to anyone except a lady from Cameroon named Blessing. My only words to her were, "Does coffee affect pregnant women?" She told me pregnant women should avoid coffee, so I didn't drink any.

The following morning during registration, I told the volunteers that I was pregnant, but I assumed I had lost the baby because of the bleeding.

They sent me to get a test and ultrasound right there in the camp. I was so happy to learn that I was still pregnant despite the continued bleeding. The medical staff administered many other tests. I was positive for anemia but negative for HIV and other sexually transmitted diseases and infections.

They asked me, "Do you want to keep the child?"

"If I don't want to keep the child, why do you think I am here?" I exclaimed.

They put the ultrasound probe on my belly, and suddenly I heard a *dub dub dub* sound coming from the screen.

I asked, "What is that?"

"It's your baby's heartbeat!" they told me.

When I heard that living, beating heart, I knew I was no longer alone. I had someone to protect, and my heart swelled and overflowed with a fierce love for the baby inside me.

Isn't God wonderful? Even though I continued to bleed from my time in Turkey until I was seven months pregnant, my child somehow wasn't affected.

At first, I worried that the camp was another trafficking organization because I saw so many black people there and suspected they had been trafficked like me. However, the people who saved us from the sea were kind, and no one tried to force us to go anywhere against our will.

I sat outside the tent in camp at night, reflecting on my life. I had been so busy in Turkey and Nigeria with clients that I couldn't ever just take time to think.

As I took the opportunity to sit and think, the whole night passed and felt like only a short time. I didn't speak to anyone but sat mutely, meditating on my life and experiences and pondering my questions. Before I had reached any conclusions, it was morning already.

I kept asking myself, "How far must I run so Madam Malus can't see me? Where can't she operate? With her power and influence, am I safe here?"

And the only answer that came to my mind was always,

"NO.

NO.

NO.

YOU CAN'T RUN, AND YOU CAN'T HIDE."

Satan, shame on you for those endless lies. I know the battle is not over, but fear no longer controls me.

Then I met a white girl, Gracia, who was working as a volunteer with an organization in camp. She is a serious Christian, a lover of people, and a carefree and free-spirited lady. She is often so busy taking care of everyone around her that she often doesn't care for herself, especially her hair, which is usually messy.

Gracia first approached me when I was outside and said, "Follow me to section C." She offered to help me carry the blanket they gave us when we slept outside. She is a fast worker who moves with incredible speed.

I was watching her and thinking, *She's so tiny! The wind could blow her away, but she walks faster than the wind.*

I was sitting outside the new arrivals tent with some Dominican women. A group of African women went into a large tent together, and I was with them. Gracia was so happy that I could speak English and asked me, "Are you alone? Do you have a family?"

I only told her, "That's a long story."

Gracia didn't have the room for the pregnant women ready, so they put me into a tent. I would have to sleep on the ground even though I was pregnant and bleeding. However, I accepted the tent gratefully because my only desire was my child's safety. Comfort didn't matter to me.

As I was lying in the tent, trying to stay warm in the winter weather, I sang in my terrible singing voice:

"You are great, yes, you are
Holy One
Walked upon the sea
Raised the dead
Reign in majesty
Mighty God
Everything written about you is great."[1]

As I sang, Gracia came and said, "What's your name? You are not supposed to be here, because your profile showed you are pregnant."

I immediately recognized those words, but I didn't remember that they were from my dream years before in Nigeria.

"Have I heard your voice before?" I asked in surprise. God knew I needed that dream to recognize and trust Gracia. I realized just then that I had been transported to the place of my destiny like Joseph in the Bible.

Gracia said, "Wait; I am coming right back."

When she returned, she said, "Follow me," and took me to a room with a bed and a heater. She did all this for me—a common prostitute, a dirty person, a foolish girl, a condemned outcast, a pregnant, bleeding lady.

---

[1]Crown, Steve. "You are Great." *You are Great*, Asylum Records UK, 2014.

Thank you, Gracia. This is why I call her my Grace of God on earth.

Gracia poked her head into the door later, and I was kneeling on the floor, praying and thanking God for the warm place. After she left, I thought about Gracia's familiar words and asked myself how this could be. Had I been here before? What was going on? I reflected for quite a while before realizing that Gracia was the woman from my dream in Nigeria when I was a little girl.

CHAPTER 12

Salvation

All my experiences with witchcraft and voodoo made me sensitive to the presence of evil, so my stay in camp was hell for me. Evil hung over the place because of all the immorality and sin there. This was not good for me while I tried to escape my past spiritual entanglements and hadn't yet found deliverance.

While I was at the camp, I struggled to sleep at night. While in the brothels, we were forced to sleep without clothes to facilitate rape— anyone daring to disobey would be strangled with their clothing. Now that I was sleeping with clothes on, I couldn't relax for fear that they would be used to choke me. These traumatic memories, coupled with stress and anxiety, made it difficult to sleep in peace.

One day, being totally under the devil's control, I had a severe spiritual attack, and I tried to kill my child and myself. The psychologist came to try to calm me down to no avail. My friend Blessing entered the room and got right into my face saying, "Fight them, FIGHT them in the name of JESUS!"

I managed to whisper the name of Jesus and was immediately released from the spiritual attack.

Even while awake, I experienced numerous intense spiritual attacks as Madam tried to regain control by invoking her power over me. I felt my name being called several times, especially at 2:00 a.m. Sometimes I was unaware of what was happening, and witnesses described me in a trance, hitting my stomach, trying to kill my unborn child.

I kept seeing a woman who ordered me to follow her and obey her instructions. She addressed me as Sarah, as I was known during my captivity. Once, she told me to jump into the sea, so I obeyed, unaware of what I was doing, just wanting to die peacefully. Some people were nearby in a boat, and they hurried to rescue me from the water. After they pulled me onto the beach, some volunteers came to help.

They took me to the hospital, and I eventually returned to Section C at the camp, but I didn't feel safe. Madam would stop at nothing to capture me, so why shouldn't I just call her and surrender? I wanted peace, and turning myself in seemed like the easiest option. I knew how things worked in Madam's world; if she couldn't kill me, she would try to kill people I cared about. I had finally found friends in the camp who loved me and whom I cared about very much, and I didn't want them to suffer because I continued to defy Madam Malus. The volunteers at the camp were the first people who ever gave me something without expecting anything from me in return.

Amazingly, I was still pregnant, despite the efforts to induce an abortion in Turkey with herbal concoctions, pills taken orally and inserted vaginally, trauma, beating, gang rape, starvation, and stress. Although my bleeding lasted for seven months, I continued carrying my child simply because I asked God for freedom.

Having a child represented both a threat and the freedom I was reaching for. Every time I held someone else's baby it triggered a battle inside. I felt that I wasn't supposed to have a child since that was so dangerous in the domain of human trafficking. Having a child represented both the past I was running from and the future I was afraid of.

My bleeding continued, and the medical staff couldn't do anything to stop it. The midwife told me she didn't know where the blood was coming from.

Once, in agony, I told Gracia, my good friend and sister from America, "I just want to sleep and rest like my mother, but no one gives me tablets. I just want to rest. My heart is so heavy." Sometimes the emptiness was so deep I thought my baby was no longer inside me.

Gracia never gave up on me, even when I tried killing myself or sent her away. She never despised me and showed me the love of a sister and a true Christian. She constantly reminded me that my sins could be forgiven. I knew she was too innocent to believe some of the terrible things I had been involved with, but she insisted it didn't matter what I had done. She just kept loving me, and on the 29th of December 2017, when life seemed the worst, she came to be with me and share my pain. She quoted some verses to me from the Bible and then asked if I knew how Jesus died.

"Before He died", she said, "they beat Him and stripped His clothes. He saw the cup of suffering He would have to drink to pay for your sins so long ago. They were forgiven that long ago."

Using verses from John, Matthew, and Isaiah 40, Gracia finally persuaded me that my sins were truly paid in full. For the first time ever, I found the faith to believe it was true.

The following day, I went with Gracia to pray with Pastor Edward. When I prayed, I didn't confess the sins that haunted me the most because I didn't want to defile Gracia's innocence by naming them. I didn't want her to hate me, and I wanted her ears to still be holy. I prayed for forgiveness, confessed some of my sins, and was partially relieved. Still, I felt that I hadn't been released from my big sins. Despite the relief I felt, the battle was far from over.

I cannot give praise to anyone except God. He had to work hard in my life, so His name will always be praised. Even as I recognized God's grace in my life, I still could not believe that He could forgive my massive sins in a twinkle of an eye.

A lady from an anti-trafficking organization came to interview me once. I was worried when I heard that she was from South Africa because that was one of Madam Malus' bases. I wore a hat and wrapped a scarf around my face so the lady could only see my eyes. I was terrified that this was all a trick and Madam was somewhere in the camp.

Finally, I couldn't take any more of the constant fear of being captured and returned to the life I had fled. I locked the pregnant women's room and tried to hang myself and my unborn son from an electric cord in the room. It took two hefty African women and Kalee, one of the volunteers, to break down the door and undo the noose around my neck.

After that, I fought spiritually, trying to get free of the fear that haunted me. I had a dream one night, so vivid that I got up early and walked the long way from the camp to the village where Gracia lived so I could tell her about it.

I told her I had dreamed that two people were trying to get me to follow them. The one on the left grabbed my arm and tried to pull me after him while saying, "Follow me!"

The one on my right was more gentle and quietly urged me, "Come after me."

At the same time, a voice that sounded like Gracia's told me to follow the gentle nudge to the right. I was yelling at the forceful one on the left to leave me, but he was pulling so hard my arm physically hurt when I awoke.

I told Gracia about the dream, explaining that I didn't know what it meant. She took me to see Pastor Edward, and I was so nervous. While in his house, I saw a python outside the window and heard Madam ordering me to leave the house.

Gracia noticed I was restless and fidgeting, and I told them I needed to leave. I knew Madam could hurt innocent people, and I was afraid she would hurt Pastor Edward and Gracia.

Before I met Gracia, I had certain assumptions about white people, but she was not like I imagined. She cared for people so unselfishly that she often neglected taking care of herself. Christianity is not proven by your mouth but by your actions. Gracia showed me and many others that practical Christianity means extending your hands to the rejected, heartbroken, frustrated, sick, and helpless.

Why wouldn't I want to be a Christian with a girl like Gracia as my example? Christianity does not mean a church background. It's having your hands extended in kindness to your brothers and sisters, serving them as you would serve Jesus Himself.

I wrote this in my journal:

2017 is on its way home where 2018 will appear, and all my past years will never be remembered again… God refused me to stay there for another year, which will be my 12th year of suffering, slavery, prostitution, and other evildoing and practice.

No one could have dragged me out of that world, but to protect my child, I had found the strength to take a step. I had only asked God to set me free from slavery and prostitution, not to spare my life. I fully expected to die because no one survives after escaping from Madam Malus. My only consolation was the thought that at least I would die free from evil and prostitution.

I had done many things I was now ashamed of, from every conceivable sexual activity to selling babies. While in the brothel, we slept with people who called themselves pastors. We brought down political opponents of my Madam's clients with sexual blackmail or murder.

Yet my pregnancy remained, and it baffled me how this was possible. The same medication that had triggered so many abortions in me earlier just did not work this time. How was this possible?

The midwife took an ultrasound and said the baby was forming perfectly.

She gave me ultrasound pictures, and I felt like I was dreaming. The photo gave me powerful hope and proved that my baby was alive and well. He was a boy, and he was smiling.

CHAPTER 13

Traffickers in Camp

Even after trusting God to forgive my sins, I didn't feel safe in the camp. I still didn't understand that God's power can smash through barriers and break the spiritual chains that Madam Malus had bound me with. Thankfully, I hadn't memorized Madam's number, or I would probably have called her and given myself up. Often, I felt the urge to do that as the easiest way out.

I didn't sleep well at night and learned to keep one eye open in case of threats. Trying to get comfortable, I sometimes moved from the top to the bottom bunk. I felt exposed and vulnerable with all the women in that section going in and out constantly.

One night, a woman crept up to the bed where she thought I was sleeping and stabbed the mattress where she expected me to be. I screamed and attacked her, but everyone else in the section said I must have been dreaming. I had no idea why the woman wanted to kill me.

When I reported the attack, I learned that the lady I identified as the attacker had left the camp. In my desperation to leave camp,

I was even tempted by the promises made by traffickers outside the gates. Meanwhile, I asked for extra gate guards at the door. Gracia tried to identify the lady through her file, but she had disappeared from camp. Why would she want to kill me? I was so afraid. The psychiatrist told me I was having psych problems, but I knew the reality about my traffickers. They can't bear to lose money. Money is their blood, and they're unwilling to lose even one person.

Do you know how heaven rejoices when it gains a soul? If hell loses a soul, imagine the opposite reaction.

One of the Greek women in camp even asked me, "What is so special about you that they want to kill you?"

The traffickers in the camp invited me to come with them, promising to take care of my documents and find a job for me. Sadly, some people living in the camp are trafficking women in that way. You run from one organization into the arms of another, worse than the one you escaped from. The people outside the gate didn't know I was an expert in trafficking. They offered me a job, telling me they would help me leave, but I knew the truth.

One day Gracia came, and I smiled and told her I would deport myself and go back to Madam Malus. I told my volunteer friend, Kalee, that I would call Madam, and that a lady I knew in Turkey was messaging me for help. I was indicating that I was going back to my old life.

That night, I went to Gracia's house and watched "Nefarious, Merchant of Souls", a movie about the sex trade. I told Gracia afterward, "I will never go back to Madam, and I WILL start a rehabilitation home!"

My emotions swung back and forth like that all the time. First, I thought I would return meekly to Madam, and then I thought I would spend my life fighting trafficking. Where did I belong? Would it be better to go back to the familiar horrors of the past?

I told Gracia I had always wanted freedom, but what am I free to do? I don't belong to anyone, and I don't even know for sure where I came from. Madam had promised me frequently that I would go to America and be free. I hadn't been the head of house in Turkey, but Madam kept promising me that I would soon go to America and work for myself.

Gracia was so upset when I told her about Madam's promises to me. She retorted in her high-pitched voice, "That's a lie from the pit of hell!"

I know now she is right; Madam would never have freed me. Why would she ever set me free if she wouldn't sell me for cash to the man who tried to buy me?

The place Gracia referred me to was an organization that helps survivors of sex trafficking. They came to the camp and offered to help me, but I was afraid as I remembered how Madam worked with many different organizations, pretending to do good.

Nothing was ever free in my world. Everything had a price; whether knowingly or not, willingly or not, freely or not, everything had its price.

I didn't know what a gift was. I only knew business, an exchange of equivalent value, so I refused to believe the organization. Gracia was convinced they were good; Kalee was sure they were trustworthy, but I was suspicious. These two Americans didn't know the reality of my old world. They both had good lives. They knew about the thing called *trust*, but I didn't know or believe in it.

They had families who loved them, but I didn't. When they believed in the organization, I laughed and told myself they couldn't understand but decided I wouldn't spoil their innocent minds. I felt that Gracia and Kalee were like toddlers who didn't know the real world, so carefree and trusting. Gracia felt sad that I wouldn't go, but she told me it was my choice.

I just said, "Sorry, I can't go with them."

At this point, I still didn't know how to trust, but I knew God had connected me to my friend, Grace of God on earth, to help me learn to trust. I liked Gracia very much, and I trusted her, but I still didn't trust a private organization. She was optimistic and sure that they would take good care of me, but I thought she was too innocent and trusting. Still, I knew God had connected us through that dream from my childhood (not that I truly believed in God or trusted Him to protect me at that time).

I had a dream where two women told me they would kill me if I didn't follow them. One day, as I was returning from church, I saw the women from my dream outside the gate. They threatened that if I didn't follow them, they would harm my friends in the camp. I thought of Gracia, Blessing, and Kalee, and I wanted to protect them from harm.

I agreed to follow the two women who had threatened me, and that's when I jumped into the water to kill myself. I told Gracia she wouldn't see me again, and I walked to the sea and jumped in to drown myself and my child. A Syrian man saved me, pulling me out of the sea. I had purposely gone to a deserted area, but this man appeared from nowhere and pulled me out of the water.

He told me, "Don't try that again."

A YWAM van full of volunteers passed me while I was in the middle of the road. They stopped and tried to help me, urging me to calm down.

Calm down for what?

You can't threaten a dead person. I thought if I could just die, Madam wouldn't have any further business with me.

I had a dream in which I was bleeding, sitting in a cage with a baby lion and my mother. The baby lion tried to open the gate to leave, but my mother stopped him. It became angry and roared when Mother closed the door.

In Genesis, Jacob blessed his son Judah and said, "You are a lion's cub, Judah," because his descendant, the Lion of Judah, would come to bring freedom to the earth. My dream showed me that my son was like a lion's cub, fighting for freedom and justice in my story.

When I woke up, I had a lot of blood. I went to Mama Blessing for help. She was a Cameroonian woman who took pity on me and treated me like a daughter, feeding me and caring for me like her own. The first time we met, I had just arrived from Turkey and asked her about drinking coffee while pregnant. Mama Blessing told me I shouldn't drink coffee, so I didn't.

One day, I went down to room 10 and saw Blessing cooking outside. I asked her if I could pay her to cook for me. From that day forward, she cooked and brought me food for free. I had only given her five euros, but she never stopped bringing me food. She still cares for me today like a mother and is like my late mother, not afraid to correct and scold me when I need it. Mama Blessing started protecting me even though she didn't know my story.

The two women who had threatened me came back after I failed to drown myself. I didn't know whether they were trafficking women on their own or Madam sent them.

They said I shouldn't let anyone know where I was going, so I left without a word to my friends in the camp. The two women boarded the ferry with me to go to the airport in the city. I had already received my travel card, so they didn't question me when we boarded the ferry. I cooperated with them, afraid to resist for fear of endangering my friends in the camp.

When we arrived in the city, we stayed at a house near the port for a short time. I called Gracia one time and told her to pray for me. She did not know what was happening or where I was.

The women told me that we had a flight booked to Germany, then to Spain. I was supposed to follow them and do whatever they did.

When we went to the airport, the black lady walked in front of me, while the white woman was at my back.

I kept thinking, *I have to outsmart these people, but how?* I was pregnant and desperate to save my son, but I had no clue what to do until the airline employee said, "Enjoy your flight" in the hallway.

That's when I saw some policemen without uniforms. I was so afraid, trying to make eye contact with the security people to give them a sign of distress, but they were unaware. One just nodded at me as if wishing me a pleasant flight.

In desperation, I pinched the hand of one of the policemen to get his attention. The lady behind me kept walking down the hallway. The man asked me what was wrong, and I told him I couldn't say, but someone was trying to take me against my will.

The police took me from the airport to the police station and asked me many questions. I knew nothing about the women who tried to traffic me, so I couldn't answer most of their questions. They offered to take me back to camp, but I told them to take me to prison so I would be safe. They denied this request, but when they saw by my documents that I was pregnant, they took me to the emergency room at the hospital.

The police didn't believe at first that I was pregnant because my bump wasn't big, even though I was six months pregnant with a boy. The officers were very kind to me, and I asked to call my friend.

I called Gracia, and she talked to the police. I sobbed and told her they would take my baby and that I was at the airport. When Gracia had come to the camp that morning and saw that I was missing, she called the police and the United Nations and gave them my information.

Back in the tiny cell in the police station, I slept very well and felt safe because the police had guns, and I knew they would protect me. I wanted to stay there, but I had to move on. The police gave me their number to call if I had any problems and took me to a big hotel in the city. Then they called the anti-trafficking hotline in Europe, and they connected me to an organization for women. I stayed in the hotel for some days until the organization sent a taxi to bring me.

Freedom and healing are not easy; they are found step by step. I know that freedom is difficult because I was trafficked as a child—but I also knew that if I could be free, so could anyone who heard my testimony.

The people in the organization that took me in were very kind, and the staff was there to help the trafficked women plan their future. It is wrong to only help people based on your agenda as if it were a business. I wanted to work, but some people are enemies of progress and would simply keep the girls in a house with nothing to do. This is one reason why many girls go back to prostitution. I would have been willing to stay there longer, but I wanted to see Gracia and Mama Blessing again.

Gracia kept reminding me about the other organization for women, but I refused to go because it was a private organization. I knew all about some Nigerian private organizations that functioned like a business rather than a ministry.

I kept rejecting Gracia's imploring for a long time, but I knew she would never deceive me; if she said it was safe—I could trust her.

"Let me try them," I said at last. God was moving me from place to place for His purposes, like Joseph in the Bible.

Up until now, no one knew why I had left the camp or that I feared for my friends' safety. A social worker had been assigned to me by then, and I told her I was going to an organization for women.

She asked if I was sure, and I said, "Yes since my friend Gracia is sure, I am sure too."

My social worker said she would take me to the organization herself and see the house and the people in charge.

CHAPTER 14

Stephen

After I decided to go to the organization for women, my social worker took me there, and I moved in. An American girl named Candice was living there. The house was in a good area, the apartment was nice, and there was maximum security inside. The organization empowers the girls by teaching them Greek and other basic courses like management and handcrafts.

One day, my water broke without contractions or pain. I was terrified that someone would take my child from me after delivery and falsely tell me that he died, as some Nigerian organizations did. I was scared to deliver my child at the hospital, but when my water broke, Anna, one of the staff, urged me to go to the hospital. She explained that my baby might not survive without the water.

When I got to the hospital, the staff decided I needed a Cesarean section.

I thought, *These people want to use my brain. They want to inject me to put me to sleep and take my baby away. No way am I allowing them to do that to me.*

When the nurses said it was time to go to the operating room, I refused. When they asked why I wouldn't go, I told them, "I know what you know!"

"What do we know?!" they asked.

"You want to take my child!" I said.

"Why would we want an African child?" they demanded.

"Because you want to sell the child!" I said.

I noticed that when white people get frustrated, they turn red. The hospital staff was very red as they talked in Greek, and I finally agreed to the operation because they asked me if I wanted to save my baby or not.

They promised they wouldn't inject me and explained that I would only be sleeping from my waist down. Part of me said to believe them, but another part warned they were trying to trick me, so I called my friend Gracia and asked her what I should do. Gracia said I should trust the hospital staff and agree to the Cesarean. She also told me that my friends were praying for me.

Auntie Anna from the organization for women was there with me the whole time, doing all the paperwork and running from place to place. I felt reassured by her presence and support, so I agreed and went to the operating room.

I started to see and hear people whom Madam had killed. They were calling for me to join them, and I didn't know how to pray in this situation. I had known all of them when they were alive, and I knew how all of them had died. They kept telling me to come to them.

"Wait for me," I said. "I'm coming soon."

I told them to wait for me because I wanted to see my baby before joining them in death. The doctor asked me some questions, but I wasn't responding to him, only to the dead people.

Suddenly, I heard a baby cry, and someone was tapping me, trying to show my son to me. I could hear them speaking, but I was sure I would join those dead people. No one survives running away from Madam, especially pregnant.

They gave me an injection, and I felt cold and was shivering. When I opened my eyes, I saw a tiny baby close to my face in the operating room. I felt butterflies in my belly as I gazed at my precious son—it was love at first sight. I felt that my mission in life was over, and I could die in peace because I had saved my baby's life, and we were in a safe country.

I called my baby Stephen, or Chinecherem in my language, which means "God is thinking about me" or "God has me in His mind." I named him Stephen because I God for asked like Hannah in the Bible, and He answered my request.

I gently touched little Stephen's nose, and the nurses asked me what I was doing. I explained that I wanted his nose to be long and straight like Gracia's. Every time Gracia came to talk to me at night, her nose would be blocking her face, and I would tap her nose. To me, white people mean long noses and long hair.

I was in the hospital for three days, and I was so surprised to be alive. However, I knew the battle was not over. Every morning that I woke up felt like another miracle. I was numb, and it took some time before I could lift my legs. I was still afraid they would steal my baby or switch him with another one, so Anna came and took pictures of us so they could not change my child.

Baby Stephen was content and didn't cry. I had asked God to deliver me, and He used this child to rescue me because I couldn't have run this far without the motivation of a baby to save. Despite all the pills and concoctions I had been given, numerous gang rapes, and torture meant to kill my baby, he survived.

Indeed, I asked God, and He answered my prayer.

I had to go back to the organization without Stephen because he had jaundice and needed to stay in the hospital a while longer. I was afraid to leave him there and wanted to wait for him. I started crying, and when I came home, I didn't eat. In Nigeria, you never come home from delivery without a child unless the child has died. I thought that my Stephen was dying, so I was restless and didn't do anything.

When I awoke the next morning, I walked straight from the organization to the hospital without bathing or brushing. I had a C-section only three days before, and I had no money or bus ticket, but I didn't even feel pain as I shuffled along in my slippers. If you are a mother, you will walk over needles for your child.

At last, I arrived at the hospital, and they finally gave my son to me. I knew I would never leave him again, and we have never been back to the hospital except for vaccinations since then. I learned to trust the hospital more since they didn't take my baby and sell him.

When I got back to the organization with my baby Stephen, I felt wonderful. My baby didn't cry, and he didn't stress me. I started asking around for a family to adopt my son to have a good life. Anna asked me many times if I was sure I wanted to give him up for adoption. At the time, I felt certain because I was full of wounds, and I didn't want my son to grow up with such pain. I wanted him to have the best life and the best family.

I didn't want him to ask the same questions I had asked as a young girl.

I didn't think I could offer him a good life. At least Stephen would know where he was born, and I didn't want to inflict my own hard life on him.

We searched for a good family for him, but nothing happened. His nose became stuffy after a few days because of the air conditioner. I ran to Pamela, one of the organization's workers, for help, and I started feeling a strong bond with my baby after this incident. I knew then that I needed to keep him and care for him myself.

CHAPTER 15

Frustration

The organization for women provided a supportive and caring atmosphere but did not allow me to get a job or work for myself. I would have to leave the safe house to get a job, but I didn't have money to rent my own place. I was frustrated that I couldn't work and that the UN wasn't giving us any money. I was angry and exasperated at the restrictions and felt that this was not the best way to help. I wanted to gather all the trafficked ladies I knew who were scared to escape or didn't know where to stay or how to survive. Instead, I was restricted to studying, but nothing penetrated my blocked brain. Not everyone can sit in one place and learn, especially when the brain is blocked from excessive trauma.

Each person should be encouraged in what they want to do, whether that's work, school, learning skills, or starting a business. How can someone begin a new life if they don't have the money they need? Those willing to work should be empowered to do that for their future. We all have different ways of moving forward because we have unique challenges and need varying solutions.

Some programs feel like more incarceration, in my opinion, and the rescued women will do whatever they're told because they have nowhere else to go. No matter how good the intentions may be, the result is that the women still feel trapped and enslaved.

Despairing, I had many thoughts that distorted my reality, and everything began to frighten me. I knew Madam wasn't worried about losing girls, even if they met someone who helped them escape because she still had spiritual control over them.

One girl I knew ran away with a client. The man came to Madam Malus and asked how much was needed to pay her off, and Madam asked for $50,000. The man did not have that much money, so the girl ran away with him. She began bleeding and came back to beg Madam for mercy but ultimately bled to death.

If a girl is orphaned without family, Madam will use this spiritual control to bind her. If they have family, she will kill the family members if you try to escape.

Because of my experience in the brothels, I slept without clothes on. One night, while I was staying at the organization's safe house, I had a bad dream about my past and woke up in the middle of the night. I was not in a normal state of mind, almost like I was sleep walking, but fully convinced that my dream was reality.

I put on my robe and left the house with Stephan in my arms, setting off the house alarm. Candice and Pamela heard the alarm and ran upstairs to check on me. Seeing that Stephan and I were missing, they searched outside and saw me walking down the street. When they caught up to me, I was terrified thinking they were evil people trying to chase me. I collapsed in the middle of the street and they called an ambulance for help. As they helped me up, I begged them not to take Stephan away from me. They assured me that they were not going to hurt us and convinced me to come home.

Back at the house, I was still not in a normal state of mind. When the ambulance and the police arrived, I screamed in pure terror when the authorities approached me and hid in the back yard. My robe fell and, in my nakedness, I screamed holding on to my baby with all my life.

Pamela started to call me by my African name and Candice convinced me to come upstairs and see the photo of my mother, which she knew I kept in my Bible. Their words got me back to my room safely with Stephan. The next day, I did not remember what happened.

Then, another terrifying incident happened. My mind was so confused that one day, when I saw a caterpillar on the balcony, I thought it was a snake. I had a phobia of snakes because Madam had put a spiritual snake inside my body, making me terrified of them. I didn't know it was only a caterpillar, so I ran around the house yelling that I was dying and screaming about the snake.

Candice brought a broom and, when she saw the caterpillar, she told me it was not a snake. Still, I kept screaming hysterically. I gave Stephen to another girl who lived in the house and got a knife from the kitchen, threatening to hurt myself. This girl ran to get help and Pamela came to calm me down. After she got the knife away from me, I took Stephan and ran away again to a nearby park. Still in my distressed psychological state, Pamela tried to convince me to come back to the house, where I would be safe. However, the situation escalated and I was it was clear that something was really wrong with me the last few

days. So, the police came and an ambulance came to take me
to the psych hospital.

They wouldn't let Stephen come into the hospital with me,
so they took him to the children's hospital. He was about four
months old at the time. Pamela took milk to the hospital for my
baby, but I was so scared that I didn't even trust her anymore. I
told the hospital to test the milk because it might be poisoned.

Being separated from Stephen was equivalent to death for me.

They took scans of my brain at the hospital and told me that
I was under too much stress.

"Something is bothering you," the doctor said.

They put me on some medications, but I just wished for
death. I was talking to myself, and they saw me act even crazier.
After receiving a report from the police, they took everything
out of my room.

In the morning, a psych doctor came to see me. She didn't
speak English very well, and she had a mosquito in her face. I
told her about the insect, but she said it wasn't a problem, but I
hit her face and killed the mosquito.

"This one is really crazy!" she said.

I had told her that I didn't really have a problem, just some
stress, but when I hit her, she was sure that I did have a problem,
and she diagnosed me as mentally deranged. I learned not to
slap white people, even to kill a mosquito.

My stay in the psych hospital lasted over a month. While
there, I learned that you can be free from physical bondage while
being utterly imprisoned by spiritual control. You can also live
in self-imprisonment because of your assumptions based on
past experiences.

I could hear Madam's voice saying, "Sarah, you can't hide, you can't run. How far can you go? Have you forgotten I have you in my palm? I have your underwear, pictures, blood, and hair. Killing you is on my list, but I want you to suffer before you die."

I communicated with Madam spiritually, apologizing to her and begging her to spare my son so he wouldn't be involved in my mess. Fed up with the torture, I just wanted her to take my life and be finished with it all.

My psychiatric doctor and the nurses viewed me as an actual madwoman. I was talking to myself, shouting, and doing lots of things. Of course, none of them heard Madam's voice, but it was all very palpable for me.

The psychiatric hospital felt like a prison to me. They didn't let me go outside, and if I wanted to walk around the hospital, someone was assigned to me. Pamela visited me from the organization, and my friend Gracia traveled a long way from the camp to see me. I wasn't allowed to have any potentially dangerous objects like wires, shavers, or pens. Even soap was forbidden. They gave it to me for a shower and took it away as soon as I finished.

My social worker made an appointment for a checkup at the hospital, where the doctor ordered some tests he wanted to be performed. He told me I had some blood clots that needed to be evacuated. When I went for my appointment to have the procedure, the blood clot had disappeared, yet I was still bleeding.

Madam had warned me that I would bleed to death if I ever delivered a child. Friends and family in Christ Jesus and a group of caring believers in America kept praying for me. The doctor also gave me a pill to take, and eventually, the blood stopped. I bled for one year and eight months after delivery. Then my period ceased after only two months of being regular. Honestly, I felt so empty in my body, as if nothing was functioning. I knew God is faithful and just, and I knew He would hear my cry and heal me from the control of all the supernatural powers beneath Him. I had seen what Madam could do when provoked, and now I was a thorn in her flesh. She had destroyed 99, but I was the 100th one, and she could not defeat me.

My social worker told me she believed my spiritual battles were real, but she said I shouldn't talk about them, or the hospital staff would think I was crazy. No one wanted to accept me in their house because they feared I would kill myself.

I finally left the psych hospital and went back to the government-run safe house for women, where they support you in working or learning (for those able to study). We started the paperwork to get my son back, but it took almost a month, and I was emotionally traumatized. I couldn't sleep or eat and looked like a madwoman.

My social worker went to court on my behalf to fight to get my child back. She told them that I was stable enough to care for my son and successfully convinced the court. When she called to tell me the news, I was overjoyed.

We went together to the hospital with the court document. When I saw my baby, he looked so tiny and thin that I cried. I knew he wasn't being bathed or cared for in the way I would have done for him.

I had started bleeding again and was using diapers to soak up the blood. I felt sure I would die since I wasn't eating well and was thoroughly traumatized. They had taken the only family I had by taking away my son.

Thankfully, the next time I went to see Stephen, I was able to bring him home with me.

We searched high and low for a job for me. It was difficult for me to find work with only my asylum seeker's ID, but I managed to secure a low-paying cleaning job at a bank with my social worker's help. My salary barely covered my monthly bills as a single mother with a child, but I had to carry on.

Now that I had my own apartment, I didn't need to sleep in my clothes. My social worker tried hard to persuade me to wear clothes to bed, so I managed to do it. I had a similar experience in my apartment to the occasion at the organization for women when I ran naked into the street. I thought someone was strangling me with my clothes, so I grabbed my son and ran out into the night. This time I was lucky someone was around to help me.

My psychiatrist took scans of my brain and told me I was too damaged to work, but I left the government facility and got a small apartment of my own. I didn't know if I should be happy or not. Even today, I don't know if I should be pleased to be independent.

My freedom was unexpected; I am surprised to be alive and free and at liberty to work. Sometimes it is a problem because I am trying to build a completely different life. I feel like all of it might be a dream, and one day I will wake up in Nigeria again. Maybe this whole journey was a dream. Could this all be a dream? It feels too good to be true.

CHAPTER 16

Persistence

I have friends who are like family to me now. Family is there for you in the good and bad times; it is not always about blood relations. In Nigeria, I learned that people could abuse their own children, so having a family is not only about blood but about people being there for you. When you are down, they come to pray with you and help with your needs. Doesn't the Bible say that Jesus said those who clothe the naked and feed the hungry are doing those things to Him? Being in an international organization's safe house for women has opened my eyes. All the women in those places have several things in common: a history of trafficking, fear, lack of protection, and anger. We have questions, feel threatened, are desperate, and have been abused. The biggest thing of all is our fear of trust. We don't know who to trust or rely on. In a world of selfishness and desperation to make money, many people have sold their souls and consciences to the devil just to survive.

Nearly all rescued survivors of trafficking go back into an exploitative community for two reasons. One is because that community is their "family" and friends, the people who accept and understand them, unlike the outside world. Outsiders perceive us as dirty people, even when we leave that life and attempt to start over. We are rejected by the broader society, as most people don't want prostitutes mingling with them or their families. When we leave our life in the sex trade, we are tortured emotionally by the words and actions of people around us. No one loves or accepts us in the new life, hence why many trafficking victims return to the known and comfortable.

The second reason so many survivors return to their old lives is addiction. Some are addicted to drugs, alcohol, or money, and when they leave that world, they yearn to fulfill that addiction. If they can't satisfy their cravings in the outside world, they will go back into bondage to get it.

I was sometimes forced to take cocaine when I was working by customers who wanted extra pleasure, but I never developed an addiction. In my new life, I love Coca-Cola, not drugs.

Some women who break free realize how much money they were making for their madam, so they go back to the street to make that money for themselves. They've been trained for this work and are good at it, so they practice prostitution as a personal business.

Many women stay in the sex trade because of a threat to their families. Maybe liberation would be possible if traffickers could actually be held accountable and arrested. You can't offer freedom to someone here in Europe if that same freedom simultaneously threatens her family in Africa. The problem must be tackled at the root.

How do we get to the root? How do we address the extreme threats these individuals are living under? You can't simply pull a woman out of prostitution without understanding what led her into that life. You must know the root cause of her predicament.

When you go to the doctor with a problem, one of the first questions asked is, "How did it start?" The doctor will use that information to find out what is wrong.

Prostitution has three faces. In the first, you are forced into the sex trade against your will. Some of us didn't have a choice; we had no family or protectors. Maybe you have grown up believing the lies of the traffickers, that you are meant to do their bidding and nothing but that. You believe in them so much that they become your family, and you allow them to use and control you.

The second face of prostitution is women who try to use their bodies to ensure their future success. African society may say that a girl with more than one boyfriend is a prostitute. Such a girl might think that she may as well do real sex work and make some money since she's already called a prostitute.

A lot of wealthy married men have made young girls prostitute themselves unknowingly. They will take care of them in university, train them, buy them expensive houses and cars, and take them shopping in Turkey and Dubai. If a girl receives gifts and money in exchange for sex, what is she?

What about the very young girls married to men who already have multiple wives? Some girls below age 18 are the 10th wife of a married man. The man is rich, so she thinks he is her salvation—but he has simply bought her for his pleasure.

The third face of prostitution is the face of influence or association. One quote says, "Show me your friend, and I will show you who you are." Some people are in prostitution, not because of being forced, but because of their friendships.

A sex worker will say to a friend, "Come with me and meet my friend." When they arrive, that friend has another man with him, and the innocent girl is given to him for sex. She gets paid a lot of money for her services, and because it seems like an easy way to get rich, she starts asking when that man will come again. Soon, she's selling herself to other men too, and that's how a girl becomes a self-employed prostitute. Those girls are the hardest ones to talk into leaving the sex trade. Everything is theirs. They buy houses, recruit other women, and some eventually become traffickers themselves.

I have experienced each one of these faces of trafficking, and I believe the last is the most dangerous. These girls know what they are going into and actively recruit others into that lifestyle. You only get to keep a pittance of your earnings when working for someone else but keep all the profits when you're self-employed. This is a trap, and evil spreads. No one can talk you out of that.

When I was with Madam, I tried to save other girls from this life because I had been forced into it. I didn't try to recruit them. Instead, I would ask why they wanted to start working as a prostitute. It was always because they needed money. I would offer to help them begin a business, pay a debt, or help them take care of their families. I had to be secretive when I helped because I didn't want anyone to see what I was doing.

Now that I am free, I choose to let God take control of my life when I have money issues. I believe that my life has had many spiritual entanglements, so I have to be careful. Sometimes I want more money, and I hope to start a business, but I've never been seriously tempted to return to prostitution. I never wanted to do that work, and I performed my duties with tears and anger. Now I derive joy from the pain of making money independently. If I made money from prostitution, it would reconnect me to the spiritual entanglement of my past.

Reflecting on my life as a free person sometimes scares me rather than makes me happy. I can't quite believe that no one is raping my front and back, no one is forcing me to swallow, no one is choking me. I'm no longer being raped by a man who, being turned on by my screams, chains me to a bed and flogs me. No one is taking the money I earn from my legal and decent job.

Prostitution is not a key, but persistence is, and so is hard work. Put your hand on your heart and tell yourself that you are a survivor and a hard-working woman. I often repeat my late mother's words: "If you want to help people, help them with your hard work. Don't steal to help someone." I dream of seeing myself selling things in a shop, and I know God will bring it to realization someday. God knows that I tried to help others, and I know He will help me.

Always pray to God that you don't find yourself in a place that makes you curse the day you were born. I don't celebrate my birthday simply because nothing is good about the day I was born or the 12 years I spent on the street. However, I give God all the glory because you wouldn't know all I have been through if you met me now. God's grace, mercy, and love are upon me.

Sometimes I think about what I will tell my son when he grows up and begins asking questions.

"Mom, who are you?"

"Where are you from?"

"Where is your mother from?"

"Where is your daddy from?"

"What was your young life like?"

"What is your hobby?"

"Who is my father?"

I don't have any answers to these questions.

Every night for a long time, I had nightmares. Before I started writing my story, I was in my room with my son and had a dream or trance as I was looking out into my living room.

I saw a beast standing between my room and the living room, but I wasn't scared, and I rebuked it in Jesus' name. It immediately disappeared. As I opened my eyes, my mind flashed back to Nigeria, where Madam's spiritual advisor warned her that I would be her doom. I wondered how I, an asylum seeker in another country, could be the downfall of someone so powerful? It amazes me because, in bad dreams, I am always spiritually strong but physically weak.

I am confident that God's mighty hand is upon my life, both physically and spiritually. When my soul is discouraged, He uplifts it by sending good people to encourage me, pray for me, and meet my needs. I am accustomed to the enticing ways of evil, where things happen quickly, like magic. Now, I am learning God's way, which is gentle and slow, yet He is on time.

We all want success in life, but what does it mean to succeed in academics, business, marriage, or parenting? We need a username and password to log in to our phones, emails, or other platforms. The username of determination and the password of persistence will allow us to succeed in any of the above areas.

We also need to examine our circle of friends and acquaintances and avoid those not adding positively to our lives. The places we birth and raise our children must be chosen carefully, so they can grow up surrounded by good people. My late mother knew this and tried to avoid having people close to me, which I understand was her trying to protect me from the unknown. Even family members should not be automatically trusted, as both boys and girls have been molested by relatives. May God save us in this world.

I didn't learn much from my limited time in school, but I am learning from people around me, my experiences, my son, friends, workplace, and environment.

God has a purpose for my life, and I thank Him for my life and testimony. As God has brought good people to be my friends, I see my life slowly becoming what I dreamed of as a little girl. Despite the years of darkness and captivity, His plan for me is steadily coming true.

I am blessed to have people who support me with prayers, love, care, and provision. I have my son, Stephen. I have my friends Gracia, Kalee, Mama Blessing, and Pamela; may God favor you beyond your imagination, Pamela. You saved a life. Believe me when I say I love you. God bless you.

I have my social worker and my coworkers at my cleaning job.

Let's not forget me because I am also here to speak for myself.

CHAPTER 17

Love Calls

My favorite song goes like this:

You unravel me with a melody, You surround me with a song
Of deliverance, from my enemies, 'Til all my fears are gone
I'm no longer a slave to fear, I am a child of God
I'm no longer a slave to fear, I am a child of God
From my mother's womb, You have chosen me
Love has called my name
I've been born again, into Your family
Your blood flows through my veins
I am surrounded, by the arms of the Father
I am surrounded, by songs of deliverance
We've been liberated from our bondage
We're the sons and the daughters
Let us sing our freedom![2]

---

[2] Hesler, Jonathan David & Melissa. "No Longer Slaves." *Peace*, Bethel Music, 2020.

As the days go by, I sense my purpose in life. I won't die until God says so. Why? Because nothing happens to me without His consent. Trouble, fears, frustration, and disappointment will all come and go. Weeping may endure for a night, but joy comes in the morning.

Like Job in the Bible, my latter days will be better than my beginning. When I see a few more people set free from bondage and slavery, my joy will have come indeed.

When I first began to follow Jesus, I refused to be baptized because I had already been baptized as a child in the Catholic church. I thought it would be an overdose to be baptized again until I understood what the Bible says about baptism. With that understanding, I acknowledged that I was a sinner and confessed my sins while trusting God to forgive me.

I was baptized by Pastor Erikson and his wife, Kalee. Pamela and a few other friends were my witnesses to this special moment. I felt reborn as a new person and felt the Holy Spirit was upon me. After the baptism, I noticed that my dreams had changed. I began to have spiritual power, with which I could overcome the demonic forces. The night a beast showed up in my dream, I defeated it.

The words I used in the dream to confront the beast were the exact words that Pastor Erikson said when he baptized me. "God has given me the power to cast and bind every evil in His name, and it shall come to pass."

I said this in my dream. The beast disappeared, and I woke up.

My old identity had passed, and I felt like someone new. A passion gripped me to remove the marks from the demonic rituals that were still on my body. I wanted to get rid of the tattoo that branded me into that hellish identity, but it was a slow and painful process. Some Christian people helped pay for procedures to remove the marks made on my face when they named me Sarah. I also started removing the tattoo on my arm that branded me as Sarah under Madam Malus.

These marks needed to go because they no longer identified me. That old identity is mine no longer; God's power has superseded my past. I am now Monique or Mummy Stephen. That is who I am.

Even in all the horror of my old life, I had access to all the material things I wanted. After my rescue, I was often penniless. Even when the devil speaks to me with Madam's voice, reminding me that I am cashless and suffering, the love of God and the love of my mother defeat those words. If not for the help of my Savior, what could I have possibly done?

Once, my mother asked me whose report I would believe in my life, and I said, "It is the report of God."

She said, "Bravo."

Since I believe the report of God and will prove the devil wrong in my life, God will prove Himself. His will for my life includes:

1. I shall live to declare His goodness in the land of the living
2. A good life and good health
3. Fruitfulness
4. Prosperity
5. Success in every endeavor
6. Protection
7. Upliftment
8. God's grace
9. Love
10. All good things shall be added unto me

Satan opposed all these words for my life, but God proved him wrong in His infinite mercy. Only the living person writes a will, so Jesus came in the form of a human, born to a woman, but Satan has no mother. For Jesus' will to be read, He had to die. Because of the love He has for me and to deal with the corruption in the world, He died. But after three days, He rose from the dead to supervise the reading of His will in my life. What further evidence do I need of His love for me?

I challenge Satan whenever he suggests that God doesn't love me or that His plans over me are not good. I came to realize that LOVE conquers every situation in life. Since I love God and my late mother, I should hold to their words because He who loves can never disappoint you, especially God.

Even if I had to stay in the camp forever with no money, I would not desire my past life, even though I wore gold back then to impress my clients. I would gladly wear rags and please my God, the owner of all creation. He is more than a billionaire, and He won't let me go empty-handed as a child of God.

Oh yes, I believe.
I believe in only one God.
I believe in Christ Jesus.
I believe He died for my sins.
I believe in total redemption.
I believe He will accomplish HIS will in my life.

The devil imprisoned me in a dark place, telling me that God couldn't forgive all I did, but those were lies from the pit of hell. God sent His grace through Gracia to put me back on track because I was perishing out of ignorance. Here I am, back on track, looking upon the cross of Calvary where He said IT IS FINISHED.

Indeed, it is finished.

Devil, you are heartless, and with the grace of God upon my life, I will rescue people from your captivity and restore them to where they belong. Although you and your cohorts put all kinds of marks on my body, it now belongs to a new landlord. He is jealous and will not share me with anyone. He is a consuming fire, and whoever He frees is free indeed. My life story is a testimony, and I overcome you by the blood of the Lamb and the words of my testimony.

I am now free, and my next step is accumulating the weapons to fight spiritually. I will establish my restoration home. It has surely ended in praise in my life.

I knew the Word of God before, as a child, and I believed in God, but something was lacking in my Christianity. Gracia brought back the faith that had died within me during 12 years of slavery. The Bible says that people perish for lack of knowledge. I would have certainly perished for lack of knowledge that my sins could be forgiven. My deeds and lifestyle seemed to be beyond forgiveness until that fateful day when Gracia helped me understand the gravity of the death of our Lord Jesus Christ. She didn't stop there and took me also to gatherings where they prayed and preached. Many things resulted because we battle not flesh and blood but principalities and powers in high places.

Satan never rests, but God will have mercy upon whom He will. Just ask me; He picked me out of dirt and sin and cleaned me up from the worst offenses. I know we live in a sinful world, but accepting Christ and believing He died for me was the best thing I have done in my entire life. The battle has not ended, but I pray that I never falter in this heavenly race.

Though I have no biological family, I have the greatest Father of all: the Faithful One, the Lily of the Valley, Author and Finisher of our faith, THE SAVIOR, the Help of the needy, and the Merciful God. He is the Almighty, for one with Him is a majority. He is everything.

Thank you, Jesus, that your thoughts are far different from those of men. You are the definition of perfect. My late mother called you the God of the widow and the Hope of the needy. When I was a small girl, I called you, "Impossibility specialist and covenant-keeping God."

Only a foolish man says there is no God.

God is merciful; He picked me up and dusted me off. He accepted me wholeheartedly and showed me grace and mercy. He restored my dreams, blessed me with peace and joy, and gave me victory over my fears and the spiritual attacks in dreams.

What else could I do but return the glory to Him?

CHAPTER 18

Overcoming Power

The deeper I went into my past, the more I endangered myself spiritually. When I opened my mouth to begin telling my story, some strange things happened. At one point, Madam's threats that I would bleed to death took effect, and I started bleeding seriously. My mouth felt heavy, fear gripped me, and my countenance changed. I called Kalee and Erikson, and they came that night. We worshiped and prayed together in Jesus' name. God's mercy was on me, and Kalee was praying for me even though I hadn't clearly told her what was going on.

Suddenly, I saw a vivid vision. I was back in the voodoo shrine again, and Madam clutched my clothes to keep me from leaving. Her spiritualist came and told me his name. Then, I took the calabash pot and threw up the feces that Madam had forced me to eat. As I smashed the pot on the ground, I heard many voices praying, and I ran from that place.

I opened my eyes, looked into Kalee's face, and said jubilantly, "I am free!"

"I am really free of her. Stephen, your mother is free."

I would usually be afraid of all this, but I believed what I was told during and after my baptism—that I have power in Christ to overcome any evil. Christ's power overcomes all enemies, whether the attack is physical or spiritual, whether a dream or reality.

It's hard for me to accept when people don't understand or believe in spiritual powers. However, I don't blame white people too much because most have never been in slavery or victimized like I was. As a victim, I can sense spiritual activity by the feeling in my body, whether heavy or light.

I never celebrated my birthday, but my new friends wished me a happy birthday. Pamela wanted to celebrate my birthday with gifts because she is a kind person. I couldn't reject her kindness but, deep down, wished she wouldn't celebrate my birthday because I cursed the day I was born a million times over.

I despised the day I was born, my name, life, and actions. After all, who wouldn't? But today, I feel alive after earnest prayer over my life by Kalee, Pastor Erikson, and other Christians. I, Monique, feel alive.

I have a reason to live and can confidently say, "I shall not die but live to declare the goodness of God." I will gladly celebrate my happy birthday with a joyful heart and gratitude to God for a life story that hopefully will change someone's life. I am glad now that I was born. My scars are me, I am my story, my story is my testimony, and my testimony is an encouragement to someone.

After eating Madam's waste, I was a new person signed and sealed to spiritual bondage, but now I am a free soul since my deliverance. Therefore, I no longer have a madam, but I HAD a lady who enslaved and trafficked me for years, and she

is Madam Malus. When the Son sets you free, you are free indeed. Madam Malus has lost her grip on me, and I am sure many more victims will be set free as I have been.

I could have taken up Madam Malus's mantle and gone on to use her powers to enrich myself, but I would have sooner used my own body to make money than to exploit others. I will never follow in her footsteps. Someday I will tell her that I am well established and never used anyone to get there. She chose to operate out of the hatred she experienced and killed her own husband out of that hatred—a beast created by society, her circumstances, and her own choices.

I had never been independent before. From being dependent on my mother in childhood, I went straight into Madam Malus's exploitation. It often felt like she and the girls I worked with were the only family I had. Freedom sometimes feels like a scary dream, but I know God's plan is perfect since He is at work in me. Not only did He set me free, but He also gave me family and friends. Not just colleagues and acquaintances, but He sent pals who understand, care, and share my joys and sorrows. I no longer feel lonely now.

I am not perfect, but I am glad for the new me. I have a new life and family, so what else can I do but say, "Thank you, Jesus Christ, for all you did for a sinner like me. You picked me up from the dungeon of iniquity, cleansed me with mercy, joy, and happiness, and sweetened it with love."

I AM BLESSED. YES, I AM.

God is the reason for my joy and the melody in my heart today. I am a product of grace because many others perished before I was ever introduced into the brothel. More died during initiation and pain or while being used by politicians, yet I am alive to write my story.

It feels like just yesterday, and now my story reads like the plot of a film.

I can't believe that I can think calmly about what used to be life-threatening, and I feel fine.

God, I pray that you use me even more than I desire.

CHAPTER 19

Facing the Sun

Standing on the street one day, I realized if I want my shadow directly behind me, I need to turn my face to the light. If I want my past behind me, I need to turn my face to Jesus. He gives me supernatural power to rise above the evil and hatred I experienced, replacing them with goodness and love. He has given me the capacity to forgive the worst atrocities that have been done against me.

If a fox is caught in a trap by his tail, will he wait for the hunter to come and kill him? No, the fox will free himself by making the ultimate sacrifice, cutting off his tail. Foxes are known for their long, beautiful tails, so how will the fox feel after sacrificing it for freedom? Will he no longer be a fox? Will he worry about what the other foxes will think?

No, the fox will know that it is better to face the world with a short tail than to be dead in the hands of the hunter. It's better to tell a beautiful survivor's story than to give up and die. Our scars have a tale of sacrifice to tell.

Speaking about the shame you have carried leads to freedom. When I was pregnant, I thought I would give my baby to someone like Kalee because I didn't feel worthy of being a mother. What would I tell this child when he wondered how he was conceived? What would I tell him when he was grown?

Think about the familiar song, "Daddy finger, Mommy finger, brother finger, sister finger, baby finger..." It's a song about a complete family, and it could lead to questions from my son. He will want to know where his daddy is. Even now, Stephen is drawn to older men because he needs men in his life.

I have learned from my small sphere that many people believe in the same thing but from different perspectives. Many people acknowledge that there is something or someone with the power to affect the unseen spiritual realm. Some psychologists call it coincidence, psychiatrists call it future imagination, and I call it vision.

That brings me to the coincidence, future imagination, or vision I had at 10 years old. There is no reason I should have foreseen my life in the camp, yet I did. My mother kept me strictly protected, so I was ignorant about men and pregnancy. How could I have dreamed about living in a tent at a camp while pregnant?

In 2017 I experienced just what I had seen in my dream. That forced me to conclude that there must be a Controller of this ship we call life.

Nonetheless, the path to that incredible moment in 2017 was long and circuitous, like Joseph's in the Bible. He also saw the future in dreams, but he was sold by his brothers before they came true. Only after years in slavery and as a prisoner

did God's plan unfold just as Joseph had seen in his dreams. It wasn't a smooth journey, yet he arrived at his intended destiny.

A wounded lion is better than a dead lion. I was wounded terribly, but I am on a healing journey. It is okay to roar in pain if it means saving captives who are deeply enslaved as I was.

I saw death face to face, but it didn't claim me. I saw pain, yet it didn't drain me. Hopelessness didn't end me. Helplessness didn't lessen me. I experienced betrayal from my community, but it didn't destroy me. I saw the reality of voodoo witchcraft, yet it didn't swallow me.

I survived because my voice needs to be heard, souls need to be saved, and people need to be rescued.

Maybe you wonder whether I am still damaged from my past. The answer is yes—I have a lot of damage, including phobias. For example, I was terrified of the hospital, eating food prepared by someone else, trusting others, and of public appearances.

The tattoo given to me in the fortification process was deep and stubborn. After six painful laser removal treatments, it remained. I decided to cover it up with beautiful artwork of the Lion of the tribe of Judah. It was a painful process, but I have had deep joy and confidence ever since I covered it. I feel free. My former tattoo was like a mark of Satan that held me down, but I now feel confident and elevated above what was done against me. There is no more shame.

Some of the damage can be managed and controlled, while other things are ruined. For example, I have only one ovary and suffer from pelvic and vaginal pains because of the many rapes I endured as a teenager.

I often wear a smiling face to hide my physical pain—but my deepest pain is knowing that there is always someone else suffering what I suffered.

Yes, I am free, but I am only one out of millions.

Sometimes I suddenly lose my appetite thinking about a girl somewhere who is starving, simply because she didn't satisfy a client or earn the required amount that day. Having escaped from that darkness, how could I avoid thinking back and having such memories? I am not the last of my kind; more and more people are being trafficked without their consent every day.

I remember the first time I had the choice to sign a document if I wanted to. Having the power to choose made me feel like a baby trying to understand a new language. I struggle to make decisions even now because I was never allowed to do that during my years in bondage.

Every night, I used to need pills before I could sleep. After a long time, my system adapted to the sleeping pills, and they no longer work for me now. My eyes are often open from morning till night and then again, from night till morning. In my mind, I still hear cries and screaming.

My greatest fear is failing to achieve my dream of opening a rehabilitation center for victims of trafficking. This center was a childhood dream even before I passed through hell. Now I understand why God placed this desire in my heart as a child. I feel the frustration of not being able to help much because I have no money. Sometimes I wish I could be the wind and blow into those places and rescue the captives.

My goal is to save victims of trafficking, both male and female. Don't ask me how I will accomplish this because I ask myself the same question. Perhaps in the future, I will understand it more clearly.

Most trafficking, organ harvesting, and brothels are controlled by rich, powerful people. The owners of the brothels are well-connected politically and get away with their crimes in most African countries because of their connections or because of their spiritual power.

Confronting these people and rescuing their captives requires both spiritual power and physical means because those people have sold their souls to the darkest forces of evil. Taking them on requires financial and spiritual support.

My inability to help sometimes leads me to isolate myself so other people don't get tired of my cries of frustration. One parable says, "Someone who is being backed should not back another." I wish to be strong enough to no longer need backing from good people so I can, in turn, back someone else. When you help A, A can help B, and so on.

There are many phases of healing, so we must first understand how the wound was sustained before we know how the person can be healed.

Without a past, there is no present or future. Therefore, our past experiences prepare us for our future, and if the past didn't kill you, it can't break you. Forward ever, backward never. You can be free from the labels of your history as long as you are in the forward lane, even though your past experiences and pain were real.

The reality from the Bible is that when one is in Christ, old things are passed away, and behold, all things are made new.

Self-forgiveness, acceptance, positivity, recognition, and love are fundamental ingredients for restoration. If you have none of these ingredients, restoration is impossible.

I remember passing through a stage of self-confession to accept Christ during my baptism. Before that time, I felt only rejection, failure, self-hatred, and denial. Confessing to myself upheld me and made me feel responsible and courageous. All the positive ingredients for restoration began to fall in line from there.

It is difficult to accept Christ's forgiveness and know that He has forgiven you. Likely at least 90% of people being trafficked, whether male or female, old or young, have been subjected to spiritual rituals and forced to make oaths. They have been exposed to a power that has no mercy; the mission of Satan here on earth is to kill, steal, and destroy.

Having committed many sins viewed by many as particularly grievous, it has been difficult to forgive myself or accept God's forgiveness. When a friend tried to tell me that God would forgive me no matter what I had done, you can understand why I was skeptical.

I was thinking, *Really? How is that possible?* The same Bible that promises forgiveness also says fornication is a sin. Who knows how many men I have had sex with? They are impossible to count, from the time I was 13 years old to 23 years old.

The Bible also states that killing is a sin. Do you know how many abortions I had? I stopped counting at 18.

God said, "Don't bear false witness," but Madam made us lie against people regularly.

I couldn't even begin to number all my sins, so you can understand how difficult it is to accept that they will all be forgiven. Some sins burn the heart and leave a permanent scar.

Seducing a pastor was part of the worst order I have received in my entire life.

When my friend Gracia told me that God forgives if I confess to Him, I could not understand.

Gracia said, "My dear, He knew today would come, and His crucifixion included payment for your sins so you could ask Him for forgiveness."

I believed and confessed most of my sins, but some were too hard to verbalize until my baptism day. I prayed, fasted, and laid down my sins. Before I was baptized, Pastor Erikson asked me to repeat after him, "Monique, do you accept Jesus as your Lord and personal Savior? Do you believe that Jesus died for your sins?" I had given my life wholly to Christ now, and I was fulfilled. I felt happy and new, and I knew I had been forgiven of my entire past and was now a new creature in Christ.

It would have been much more challenging to break free if I hadn't felt such a strong connection to someone God had assigned to me in a dream many years before. We connected effortlessly, and Gracia talked directly to my heart. There is nothing that God does not know.

I felt forgiven after forgiving myself and accepting Christ. In my old life, the language I understood was an eye for an eye. We knew nothing about forgiveness.

My advice to whoever is haunted by old sins is to accept and forgive yourself. Whether you did those things intentionally or not, we've all done wrong. There is no manual for life that lets us avoid all mistakes, but we can confess our wrongs and be restored to Christ.

"But this one thing I do, forgetting those things which are behind, and reaching forth unto those things which are before,

I press toward the mark for the prize of the high calling of God in Christ Jesus." Philippians 3:13-14

If you want your shadow behind you, you must be ready to face the sun.

CHAPTER 20

A Wounded Lion Roars Again

I am full of dreams for the future. I have always thought that I want to build a hospital or a school for my mother to treat people free of charge because Nigeria has poor medical facilities. This dream started when I was very young and still with my mother.

One day Mother was coughing, and I told her, "One day, I will become a doctor so I can help people like you. I will build a hospital in your name, and people will come for free treatment."

I am not doing this for only some people, but for everyone.

When I was a child, I stole my mother's money to give to the beggars. I started my business dreaming then, as I stole and sold to give to others. I saw so many beggars, and as a little girl, I thought they should not be on the street, but they should be cared for. I wanted life to be good for everyone.

As time went on, I realized that there was a bigger challenge that could not be fixed with a school or a hospital. I learned about trafficking, and as soon as I understood what it was, I started thinking about how to help its victims. Even while forced to work in prostitution, I was planning how to help people who needed more than education or healthcare.

I had limitations at first, but when I became head of house at the brothel, like a boss, I had more freedom to help. I was helping girls without Madam's knowledge because I didn't want them to join the brothel. If one of the girls in the house hadn't made enough money for the week, I would give her enough to make up the difference. I thought my destiny was to be a prostitute, so I gave up on freedom. After a while, I was able to keep the money I was earning, so I bought clothes for the poor and helped beggars pay for a place to live. I would pay a year's rent on an apartment for someone and never regret spending the money. I cooked for the whole brothel house and invited other girls to join us.

When I escaped, I started thinking seriously of the future, dreaming about a rehabilitation home, something I would need after my escape. Sometimes women are compelled by financial hardship to return to prostitution, thinking they can keep all the money they earn if they escape their madam. I believe I would have recruited even more women into sex work than my madam had I chosen that route because of the spirit that bound me. God delivered me from that spirit of trafficking. Because of the rituals, covenants, and spiritual processes, I would be 10 times worse off if I returned to that life after God saved me. You cannot serve God and Satan; you must choose your master.

I started sketching my plans for a rehabilitation home in the camp as I lay day after day in the bunk bed in the pregnant ladies' room. I visualized myself being free for real and wondered what I would need. How could I be safe emotionally and otherwise? My dream was born out of what I needed as someone who had escaped sex slavery.

Many people and organizations have tried to help survivors, but many return to their old lives after some years because they were not given the basic necessities.

We need life after exploitation, not just shelter. We need morale—to be talked out of who we were and made to see who we can become. We need to be taught about love because we don't know what love is. We need to be taught independence because we depend on our bosses and the money we make for them. We need to learn to think about ourselves and our future and know there is a future, not just the present and the past; that is the survival circle.

My first goal in 2021 was to start a business. Slowly, God is making this goal a reality in 2022. The objective of this business is to support myself and to help others. I pass so many people who need help in my daily life, and I feel connected to them because I was there, but I feel inadequate to help. I want to open a shop and empower women to help themselves and use the income from my shop to start the rehabilitation home in honor of my mother. I refuse to use prostitution money to do this. I will start with my sweat to help people, then get a place. I have my papers now, so I can travel. I think I know now why Madam Malus's spiritual director told her I would be her downfall because I will bring her down.

I know I could help many people through business. I know what it is to be independent now. Just having my physical needs met is not enough. I need to be occupied with my passion and always be busy in my heart, doing what I know is right.

I also have a goal to help ten women this year. I want to encourage them to be independent, not hand-fed. If you give people food today, you will need to feed them again tomorrow. Don't give people fish; instead, teach them how to catch that fish. If you pay my rent today, you will have to pay the rent tomorrow. No one pays my house rent because I am working. Anything you are doing for someone needs to be seriously evaluated. You can break down if you do it the wrong way, but when you establish yourself, you can establish someone else—such is the circle of life and freedom.

A rich man is not defined by his wealth but by how many lives he has changed positively. Are you a rich man while your family and friends are poor? Then you are a poor man. We need to empower women with our money, not drain our money on beggars.

I have many challenges with my independence. People think I am connected to men because I have an apartment and pay my rent. They associate my success with men because they see me laughing in the times of my struggle. They ask my Nigerian friend if he is my boyfriend. One asked me to connect her to a man. I have temptations, but I am focused and determined. I will see to it that my passion and zeal come to fruition. With my God and persistence, it will come to pass. I will ensure that my past does not affect my present and future.

One day I will hang the sign, "Mother Tina Rehabilitation Home," and it will be a home for all. You can come as you are. Those who have worked in prostitution will be together with

the outsiders, and it will be a place where we all are united. I will personally teach about the label of prostitution because it is not a stigma; it is not our name!

It will also be a home of self-reliance. It will be a family home because too many people lack family. As I was once a victim, I came to a few conclusions of what I think a rehabilitation center should be.

Besides food and clothing, which are essential and primary, this is what people need:

1. **Family:** A once-trafficked or self-employed sex worker needs her family and those around her to see her as an ordinary person, not defined by her previous profession.
2. **Therapy:** If you want the person to overcome or leave her previous lifestyle, therapy is needed, such as talking with an expert in the field like a psychologist.
3. **Engagement:** A woman working in prostitution is always active, serving at least ten clients daily. When trying to save such a person, don't keep them idle. Instead, keep them busy doing something they're passionate about. Everyone has that one thing that makes them happy; engage them in that activity and keep them occupied. By the time they do this consistently for a few days, they will realize they haven't had clients and see they can actually have a life without sleeping with many people each day.
4. **Support:** This is essential in life. Everyone needs support from another. A yam stem needs to be braced for its growth, and so does a human. Support those who

want to further their education, careers, businesses, marriages, and families. We all have different life goals.

5. **Empowerment:** Help them move from dream to reality. It is one thing to dream and another to make it come to reality. It is usually not by hard work alone; otherwise, laborers would all be rich. Dreams materialize through a combination of grace, effort, and support. One lone tree cannot make a forest.

I have taken time to plan what the rehabilitation center will be. It won't be for ladies only, but all humankind; not for one particular country, but the whole community.

I intend to bring self-isolated and self-caged people out of their dilemmas to see the light and what they have been called to in God's purposes. Instead of hostility as in the brothels, friends will become family here.

With God's support, the Mother Tina Rehabilitation Home will deliver caged puppets from the hands of their oppressors.

I had a dream one night where I was surrounded by many evil men dressed in black in an enclosed space. I was walking around videoing what they were doing, so I would have evidence. I had all the information I needed to free many others, but I could not escape—I was enslaved. Suddenly, a large gate opened, and a magnificent lion strode through the opening. He came right up to me and crouched down so I could climb onto his back. He then turned and roared loudly to ward off the evil men trying to take me and walked majestically outside the gate where I slid off and ran with the information to free the others.

This is the Lion of the Tribe of Judah, my Savior, whose roar is majestic, His justice perfect, and His freedom rings for all to hear.

Like my mother used to say, "A wounded lion is better than a dead lion. A wounded lion roars again."

I am the wounded lion, and this book is my roar.

A Letter to Madam Malus:

I forgive you. I forgive you as a Christian. I forgive you as a mother. I forgive you as a child because you once called me your daughter. I still forgive you because you spared me when your spiritual director asked you to kill me. I forgive you because you were not born to be evil. I forgive you because you were once a victim. You became like this because of your hatred toward your father. I forgive you for your ignorance in using people to chase power and your own dreams. Growing up with you helped me understand that you have to continually use more and more powers if you want to keep them. You transferred 90% of your spirituality to me, so I know what made you change from a human into a beast. I only want you to repent and change. This wickedness is your choice. My only request is that you repent and confess Jesus as your Lord and Savior. I pray that you become the human being you once were before the lust for power and money destroyed your humanity. I forgive you totally from my heart because Christ forgave me.

A Letter to the Trafficked
Women Out There:

Please listen to me—I know your life is difficult, but don't be hard on yourself. Your true definition—that is your true you. Ask yourself, "Who am I? What am I doing? What do I desire to do?"

Ask yourself also, "What was my childhood dream?" As children, we all had dreams of becoming a doctor, lawyer, teacher, or some other honorable position. No child ever says she wants to grow up to be a prostitute. No child expects to grow up to become a murderer or a trafficker. No one aspires to be an abuser, a woman-hater, or a rapist from childhood. Yet these people created the circumstances you find yourselves in. Most likely, your society did not care about you.

Look at yourself as you see your own child. Are you proud of what you are doing? Would you be proud of your child if they followed your example? You may have been influenced by the environment, your parent's marriage, your friends, or a relative who sexually abused you. It might seem normal to acquiesce and live in this way.

I tell you, these things you are living through are your circumstances, not your identity. I beg you to find your first identity as a child—find the dream that was killed by your circumstances. Remember the light that sputtered and dimmed but was never extinguished. Walk away from the shadow that blocks your light and let it shine again. Find your true self and pick up the pieces of that self.

Therefore I tell you to view and advise yourself as to your child—you are needed, valuable, significant, and unique. Rise out of your vulnerability and speak to yourself only with positive words. Don't let your scars be a hindrance. You, and you alone, can extract yourself from this shadow.

As my friend Gracia, Grace of God, said, "Don't listen to that dark voice. It is a lie from the pit of hell!" Don't listen to the voice that says you can't be free, that you will never have a normal life. Who says so? It is a lie from the pit of hell.

Turn your negativity into positivity so you can move ahead. The devil has seen your real potential and is looking for an opportunity to entangle you. If there is no failure, there can be no success. You must fear failure to pass your examination. The possibility of failing is what makes us strive and study and work.

We shouldn't be confounded by what we have experienced. It is not a new phenomenon. Everything you are passing through, someone else has experienced before. You are not dead, so there is still hope. The hardship you are going through is not the problem. Most of us remain on the ground where we fall. We are afraid of standing up lest we fall again.

Have you seen a child learning to walk? I watched my son try, and he fell again and again and even hurt himself. But he stood up again each time and kept trying, and now he walks perfectly.

You cannot stay where you fall—you must get up. Maybe you were injured while falling, like in football, when an injured player needs a substitute. You need to rest and heal, but you are not finished!

Locate your wound and pursue appropriate healing for that specific injury. You wouldn't go to an eye clinic for help with a broken leg. And when you are healed, tell the good news to the world.

I write to you now because I believe in multiplication, and I trust that I will rise by lifting others.

I don't know what you are passing through, so I can't say
what you need precisely. Have you tried therapy or reading books?
Many people have something to say but don't know how to share
it. Some of you want to talk, but you are unsure how. The only
solution to this is to find therapy for your trauma.

A scar may be permanent, but the injury can heal. You will
have the memories, but the trauma will heal. Embrace that scar.
Let it be a part of your beauty, and nothing can be used against you
anymore. Being called a prostitute or a rapist may have destroyed
you emotionally. It may seem like it now, but prostitution is not
your identity, only your circumstance beyond your control.

Some of you stay because of fear, but take a step and leave!
Believe in God and leave with hope.

This world is full of evil, which is multiplying rapidly. Each
of us has the potential to do evil. We resist that evil as Christians
but yield to it when we are without God, and it increases. All of
us have nursed evil thoughts and done wrong. You must resist
"small" temptations before they mutate into worse evil.

God gives even wicked people a long rope to repentance.
If God dealt with us strictly by how we thought or acted, we
would all be dead. In one way or another, we've all sinned. We
all are capable of evil.

Only Christ is perfect. That is why we need to watch and
pray, to not enter into temptation. The human heart is sinful
and can germinate a bad seed. Maybe you have been through
terrible circumstances, but now you are perpetrating evil on
others. The world, this container of people, is evil. That includes
you and me, everybody.

When we accept Christ, He suppresses the evil of all this temptation around us. You cannot overcome evil alone. It is expected
that evil will come to you, but it is your responsibility to resist it.

Sometimes I'm still tempted to go back to making fast money. Do you want to go back, or do you want to move forward? Often, we don't realize that our actions always affect our future.

The wrong you have done needs to be confessed to the person you hurt. There is a difference between repentance and restitution. My mother taught me that you need to repent to God and make things right with man. The Bible says that when you want to offer something to God, first you need to make things right with your brother. The first step of overcoming evil is choosing restitution, making things right with God and others. You cannot only confess to God while refusing to make things right with people.

Believe in the God who can set you free, and renewed ways of thinking will come. God does not hold anyone captive, which means you are free to stay in bondage or walk forward into freedom. Satan binds in captivity, and Christ sets free. Choose the best thing—that is, freedom.

I have been saved by faith through Christ, and I have freedom. I could use that freedom to return to my old life and make fast money. Every day, I have the freedom to choose forward or backward. I elect to walk onward because the gift of God makes a way and adds no sorrow. I will patiently wait for God to accomplish what He has shown me in my dreams.

I was once like Job, but even Job said, "Even if worms eat my flesh, this I know, that my Redeemer lives." How could I be in sorrow for all those years in captivity and then return to despair after having tasted freedom?

Many of us taste freedom in some manner but then return to bondage. At first, you think you cannot live without the community of evil people, but what claim do they have on you?

You were born with no connection to them—your life does not belong to them!

Without being trafficked, I would not be writing as I do now. God preserved my life. Should I be angry with God for all the evil I experienced? I was once frustrated at God, but now I have made peace with Him. I realize now that God watched over me even as all these things happened. I still have my life and health. God allowed me to be transported to another place like Joseph in the Bible so I could share this message with you.

Madam Malus took me when I was young and vulnerable, but I left her and am living without her. If I can do it, you can too. You can live without them, without her, without prostitution.

Trust me, even if you are in spiritual bondage when you first choose righteousness, they will lose their hold on you, and their hands will slip off you. Whether you feel threatened by your own conscience or someone who wants to hurt you, you owe it to yourself to make the right decision. I am leading you to a stream, but I cannot force you to drink. Many people are led out of brothels, but they cannot be forced to choose a better life. I am advising you like a horse at a stream, "If you don't drink this water, you will fall, and you may lose your strength and die. Please drink this water." No one can command you to drink or force you to make that choice.

HERE ARE THREE KEY THINGS:
1. *Don't stay where you fall.*
2. *Don't let the scar of your wounds hinder you.*
3. *Move forward in the light of God.*

Support Monique's Business and Ministry!

All the proceeds from this book help Monique's future business and ministry vision. Monique started a small African food shop in the city center, and will invite women to join her there for a drink and conversation. She envisions creating a space for a restoration program for survivors of exploitation and abuse in the future.

To support her vision you can buy this book on Amazon, share her vision with your friends and family, or donate directly to Monique at

WOUNDEDLION.COM

Follow Monique's story on Instagram

@A.WOUNDED.LION.ROARS

Made in the USA
Las Vegas, NV
26 October 2022